Equality in Law between Men and Women
in the European Community

The Netherlands

Equality in Law between Men and Women in the European Community

Series Editors

MICHEL VERWILGHEN
Professeur ordinaire à la Faculté de Droit
Université catholique de Louvain

FERDINAND VON PRONDZYNSKI
Professor of Law and Dean of the Law School
Jean Monnet Professor of European Social Law
The University of Hull

SOURCES OF EQUALITY LAW

A C.I.P. Catalogue record for this book is available from the Library of Congress.

ISBN (this volume) 0-7923-1837-4 (Martinus Nijhoff Publishers)
92-826-4474-X (Office for Official Publications of the EC)

This study was commissioned by the Equal Opportunities Unit of Directorate-General V (Employment, Industrial Relations and Social Affairs) of the European Commission. It does not, however, express the Commission's official views. The responsibility for the views expressed lies with the authors.

A French version of this text has been published by the Office for Official Publications of the European Communities and Les Editions Juridiques Bruylant, Brussels.

Published by
Office for Official Publications of the European Communities, L-2985 Luxembourg
ISBN (this volume) 92-826-4474-X   Catalogue number CE-97-92-010-EN-C
and
Martinus Nijhoff Publishers,
P.O. Box 163, 3300 AD Dordrecht, The Netherlands
ISBN (series) 0-7923-1842-0   ISBN (this volume) 0-7923-1837-4

Sold and distributed for the Office for Official Publications of the European Communities by the distributors listed on the inside back cover.

Kluwer Academic Publishers incorporates the publishing programmes of D. Reidel, Martinus Nijhoff, Dr W. Junk and MTP Press.

Sold and distributed in the USA and Canada
by Kluwer Academic Publishers,
101 Philip Drive, Norwell, MA 02061, U.S.A.

In all other countries sold and distributed
by Kluwer Academic Publishers Group,
P.O. Box 322, 3300 AH Dordrecht, The Netherlands

Printed in Belgium

European Commission

Equality in Law between Men and Women in the European Community

The Netherlands

by

IRENE ASSCHER-VONK

Professor of Social Law
Catholic University, Nijmegen

MARTINUS NIJHOFF PUBLISHERS
DORDRECHT/BOSTON/LONDON

OFFICE FOR OFFICIAL PUBLICATIONS OF THE EUROPEAN COMMUNITIES
LUXEMBOURG

TABLE OF CONTENTS

COMMENTARY ON EQUALITY LAW

FOREWORD

Since the Second World War several international organizations have been endeavouring to promote the principle of equal opportunities between women and men, in law as well as in practice. This objective has also been pursued in a number of countries within the framework of domestic law. The intention has been to pursue a social objective and to achieve a change in the patterns of social conduct. In this context it has been felt that where the law visibly adopts the principle of equality this may contribute to the transformation of attitudes.

It has generally been accepted that equal opportunities ought to be pursued in the working environment in particular. In part this is because employment equality is a concept which can be more easily addressed by legal means than can other aspects of equality, but it is also true that a better distribution of wealth and income between the sexes and the abandonment of separate gender roles in the labour market can provide a powerful impetus to the realization of equal opportunities in society more generally.

To some extent these initiatives have been successful. Progress has been made in a relatively short space of time, although perhaps in limited areas of the equal opportunities agenda. But the impact has been restricted, and much effort still needs to be made in order to improve both law and social practice.

* * *

Within the European Community also there has been a steady growth of interest in the issue of equality between women and men. Article 119 of the Treaty instituting the European Economic Community, signed in Rome on 25 March 1957, provides for equal pay for women and men workers who perform equal work. The main Directive advancing the idea of equal pay, Directive 75/117/EEC, will soon be celebrating its twentieth birthday.

But it is not enough to enact Directives. It is also necessary to analyse and control the implementation of these texts in the Member States of the European Community. The Commission of the European Communities has obviously understood this, since in its Action Programme for 1982-1985 it placed particular emphasis on the need to follow up the implementation of the Equality Directives. In pursuit of this the Commission established a number of expert networks to consider the equality agenda from a variety of viewpoints. One of these networks was the Network of Experts on the Implementation of the Equality Directives, consisting of experts from each of the Member States of the Community.

These experts have drawn up a series of reports on various aspects of their remit, and have been able to offer advice to the Commission on desirable courses of action to be followed. The network has also met regularly to discuss the reports and to update the Commission and each other on important developments in each of the Member States. Some of the network's consolidated reports have been published by the European Commission, and indeed the information contained in network documentation has been used in conferences of legal practitioners and other interested persons organized under the auspices of the Commission. However, the national reports written by network members remain unpublished and are unavailable to the general public.

In fact these reports form an excellent source of legislative and jurisprudential information from the Member States in matters of equality. They shed light on the progress made and the work which remains to be done if we are to achieve equality both in law and in practice. The experts therefore expressed the desire to see their work published and widely disseminated in the European Community and internationally, so that it can be used to assist not only legal practitioners but also other groups and persons seeking to achieve the objective of equal opportunities.

However, the reports drawn up for the network could not necessarily have been published in the form in which they were produced. Their authors had drawn up working documents, rather than studies designed for publication. Furthermore network members were, at any rate initially, given significant discretion as to how the work should be produced. From 1986 onwards a common format based on agreed schemas was devised to give network reports greater homogeneity, and this also prompted a growing desire to produce a more extensive collection of knowledge in this field.

The European Commission therefore decided to promote the progressive publication of an encyclopædia on equality in law between women and men in the European Community. This was to consist of volumes which were no longer to be only administrative documents intended for Commission use, but were to present a high level of scientific and formal quality.

There is no need to discuss at length the importance and interest of such a publication, which forms a natural part of the Commission's programme of action regarding the promotion of equality of opportunity. In fact it represents an excellent method of consolidating Community knowledge of existing legal provisions in order to ensure their better implementation. It represents also the desire to extend and develop the traditional means of disseminating information, in such a way as to sensitize the public more effectively.

The plans for such an encyclopædia were formulated by experts attending the Spanish Presidency seminar on equal opportunities in Toledo in April 1989.

It was with much pleasure that the coordinators of this major project have been able to witness the gradual production of the volumes in this collection. Nevertheless, in spite of all the care take by the experts involved in this work, the encyclopædia is neither exhaustive, perfect nor definitive, since the law continues to evolve. However, it is hoped that it will prove useful to all those — judges, tribunal members, lawyers, civil servants, teachers and researchers — who are interested in this subject.

* * *

The present volume, pertaining to Netherlands law, is an integral part of the encyclopædia. It was therefore prepared on the basis of a structure common to all volumes in the series, in order to allow for a comparative reading of the law in each Member State on equality between women and men. The text reflects the position as at 1 November 1994.

The first part of the volume — the Commentary — is based on a detailed plan common to all the national volumes, drawn up in such a way as to allow the reader to adopt a comparative approach. This plan draws both on the characteristics of the legal systems in use in the States linked to the Roman-Germanic legal tradition and in those following the common law tradition. One result of this is that certain headings may not be relevant to the position in each Member State.

The rest of the volume contains legislative texts actually in force in the Netherlands which implement the principles laid down in the EC Equality Directives, as well as the most significant court and tribunal decisions applying those texts.

* * *

The coordinators wish to express their gratitude to all those who have lent their assistance and support to the encyclopædia project, and to show particular appreciation to certain of them.

We need to record our gratitude to the authors, without whom this work would not have been produced. The essential quality of the encyclopædia lies in the work of its main authors; they spared no effort in the assembling of the necessary documentation and in drawing up an intelligible and useful commentary.

A particular word of thanks is due to the staff of the Equal Opportunities Unit of DG V of the European Commission. Since the project was discussed in the initial stages a large number of officials have been associated with it and have provided active assistance and support to the coordinators. It has been a pleasure to collaborate with the Unit.

Similarly, the coordinators would like to express their sincere thanks to the officials of the Office for Official Publications of the European Communities, whose patient and expert supervision made it possible to convert the manuscripts into publishable texts of a very high quality.

We express particular gratitude to the publishing houses which accepted the burden of the present work, which is hardly lightweight as it numbers some thirty volumes!

May this work assembled with the active participation of so many eminent and committed collaborators contribute to progress in the law, to the common good and to the promotion of formal and actual equality between the women and men of Europe.

Ferdinand von PRONDZYNSKI
Professor of Law and Dean of the Law School
Jean Monnet Professor of European Social Law
The University of Hull
United Kingdom

Michel VERWILGHEN
Professeur ordinaire
à la Faculté de Droit
Université catholique de Louvain
Belgium

NOTICE TO THE READER

The editors of the encyclopædia wish to draw the attention of the reader to certain characteristics of the collection.

1. Each volume of the encyclopædia is published in two languages, English and French. The volumes have been edited so as to ensure that they have, as far as possible, the same content and structure in their English and French versions, although the language and terminology may occasionally differ as a result of normal usage in English and French respectively.

2. The authors of the Commentary section of each volume have worked according to a common schema agreed in the European Commission's Network of Experts on the Implementation of the Equality Directives. This allows the collection as a whole to follow a uniform structure. However, the Sources section in each volume is structured according to the domestic law framework, which varies from Member State to Member State.

3. The materials contained in the Sources section of each volume have (except where the original language is English or French) been translated into the two languages of the encyclopædia. These translations are not official, though every effort has been made to provide translated versions which are of high quality and accuracy. In the event of any doubt, it will be necessary for the reader to refer to legal sources in the original language; these are the only sources of guaranteed accuracy.

4. Equality in law between women and men within the European Community is a subject affected by rapid change, in EC law as well as in the law of each Member State. The formal sources evolve so quickly that information supplied in these volumes may have to be updated from that contained in the published encyclopædia. As far as possible major legislative and jurisprudential changes which occurred during the preparation of the volumes have been indicated in footnotes. The editors hope to be able to produce regular updates at a later stage.

5. References to laws, regulations and judicial decisions follow the normal usage of the Member State from which they originate.

ABBREVIATIONS

[Expressions in square brackets are translations or explanations of the relevant Dutch expressions or names.]

AAW	Algemene Arbeidsongeschiktheidswet [General Disability Act]
AB	Administratiefrechtelijke beslissingen [Administrative Law Reports]
ABW	Algemene Bijstandswet [Social Assistance Act]
afd.	afdeling (division)
AG	Ambtenarengerecht [Civil Servants' Court]
AOW	Algemene Ouderdomswet [Old Age Act]
art.(s)	article(s)
AVV	Wet op het Algemeen Verbindend en Onverbindend Verklaren van Bepalingen van Collectieve Arbeidsovereenkomsten [Collective Agreements (Pronouncement of Binding and Non-binding Provisions) Act]
AWGB	Algemene Wet Gelijke Behandeling [General Equal Treatment Act]
AWW	Algemene Weduwen- en Wezenwet [General Act on Benefits for Widows and Orphans]
BBA	Buitengewoon Besluit Arbeidsverhoudingen [Labour Relations Decree]
CAO	Collectieve Arbeidsovereenkomst [collective agreement]
CMLR	Common Market Law Review
CRvB	Centrale Raad van Beroep [appeal court]
DCA	Dienst Collectieve Arbeidsvoorwaarden [Service on Collective Labour Conditions]
EC	European Community/ies
ECJ	European Court of Justice
ECR	European Court Reports
EEC	European Economic Community
EG	Europese Gemeenschappen [European Communities]
GAB	Gewestelijk Arbeidsbureau [Regional Labour Office]
Hand.	Handelingen [parliamentary proceedings]
HOS	Herstructurering Onderwijs Salariëring [restructuring of wages in education and teaching]
HR	Hoge Raad [Supreme Court]
ILO	International Labour Organization/Office
IOAW	Wet Inkomensvoorziening Oudere en Gedeeltelijk Arbeidsongeschikte Werknemers [Act on Benefits for Elderly and Partially Disabled Employees]
JAR	Jurisprudentie Arbeidsrecht [Labour Law Reports]
KG	Kort geding [summary proceedings]
LTD	Loontechnische Dienst [Service for technical wage matters]
mn	met noot [with comment]
NJ	Nederlandse Jurisprudentie [Netherlands Law Reports]
NJB	Nederlands Juristenblad [Netherlands Lawyers' Journal]
NJCM	Nederlands Juristencomite voor Mensrechten [Netherlands Lawyers' Committee for Human Rights]
OJ	Official Journal

para.(s)	paragraph(s)
p./pp	page/pages
Prg	Praktijkgids [Journal for the Legal Practice]
Rb	Rechtbank [court]
RSV	Rechtspraak Sociale Verzekering [Social Security Law Reports]
RvB	Raad van Beroep [appeal tribunal]
RvdW	Rechtspraak van de Week [The Week's Case Law]
RvS	Raad van State [Council of State]
RWW	Rijksgroepsregeling Werkloze Werknemers [Unemployed Social Assistance Regulations]
SER	Sociaal-economische Raad [Social and Economic Council]
SMA	Sociaal Maandblad Arbeid [Labour Law Journal]
Stb	Staatsblad [Official Gazette]
TAR	Tijdschrift voor ambtenarenrecht [Civil Service Law Journal]
TK	Tweede Kamer [second chamber: parliamentary reports]
Trb	Tractatenblad [official gazette for international treaties]
UN	United Nations
WAO	Wet op de Arbeidsongeschiktheidsverzekering [Workers' Disability Act]
WIISO	Wet Interim Inhouding Salarissen Onderwijs [Act on Temporary Deduction from Salaries in Education and Science]
WROM	Wet Rechtsbijstand On- en Minvermogenden [Act on Legal Aid for Persons with Insufficient Income]
WW	Werkloosheidswet [Unemployment Act]
WWV	Wet Werkloosheidsvoorziening [Act on Unemployment Benefits]

TABLE OF LEGISLATION ETC.

[Numbers in bold type refer to pages at which provisions are printed verbatim]

Treaties, etc.

European Communities Secondary Legislation

Netherlands Constitutions

Statutes

Regulations and Decrees

TABLE OF CASES

Numerical Table of Cases

Court of Justice of the European Communities

Chronological Tables of Cases

Hoge Raad

Raad van State

Centrale Raad van Beroep

Gerechtshof

Gerechtschof Amsterdam

Gerechtschof 's-Gravenhage

Gerechtschof 's-Hertogenbosch

Rechtbank

Rechtbank Amsterdam

Rechtbank Arnhem

Rechtbank Dordrecht

Rechtbank 's-Gravenhage

Rechtbank 's-Hertogenbosch

Rechtbank Rotterdam

Rechtbank Utrecht

Raad van Beroep

Kantongerecht

Ambtenarengerecht

Equal Treatment Committee

Equal Treatment Committee for Civil Servants

Central Committee for Clerical Personnel
in Newspaper Companies

Alphabetical Table of Cases

COMMENTARY ON

EQUALITY LAW

1. GENERAL

1.1 INTRODUCTION [1]

1.1.1 INTRODUCTION TO NATIONAL LEGAL SYSTEM

Acts of Parliament and delegated rules (i.e. rules made by institutions or people who have been given authority by an Act of Parliament to do so) cover many important areas of the Dutch labour relations system. Among these areas are safety at work, job security, minimum wages, collective agreements and works councils. Sometimes the rules are of a mandatory nature, sometimes they are supplementary. It is part of the Netherlands legal tradition to include custom as one of the sources of law. However, as far as labour law is concerned, most issues are covered either by statute or by collective agreement. This means that the scope for custom in labour relations is a narrow one.

After statute law, collective agreements are the major source of labour law. In fact, it can be argued that for the majority of workers collective agreements are much more important than statutory protection.

According to Dutch legal theory, decisions of the courts are not officially regarded as a source of law. Nevertheless, in practice the decisions have far-reaching effects on judges and citizens alike. Therefore, whatever the theoretical position, the decisions are, *de facto*, an important and integral part of the legal system.

Labour law comprises the rules which regulate the relations between employer and employee and between their respective organizations. This description includes employees and their organizations in the private sector as well as those in the public sector. In practice, however, labour law concentrates almost exclusively on the private sector. This means that the status of civil servants is uncertain, positioned between labour law and administrative law. Equal treatment law, however, is applicable both to civil servants and to private sector employees.

The following subjects are generally seen as being the most important within the field of labour law:

---

[1] For this introduction, extensive use is made of H.L. BAKELS' contribution to the *International Encyclopædia for Labour Law and Industrial Relations*.

(a) the rules relating to the working environment within the enterprise, such as rules concerning maximum working hours, safety and health; these are rules of public law, and as such they are backed up by criminal sanctions;

(b) individual labour law, which focuses on the contract of employment, the rights and duties of the individual employer and employee, dismissal law, and problems of a similar nature;

(c) collective labour law, which includes trade union law, collective bargaining, collective agreements, strikes and institutional participation (i.e. the participation of workers' representatives through works councils and supervisory boards); and

(d) social security law.

Social security legislation was originally linked to the concept of the contract of employment: it protected employees against certain risks, such as occupational accidents, illness and disability. In the years since World War II, however, a far more extensive social security system has been developed which, in many cases, extends its benefits not only to employees, but also to all residents of the Netherlands. This extension has loosened the ties with labour law. Furthermore, the social security system has developed its own (highly complicated) administrative machinery and its own tribunals for administering justice. All of these factors when taken together encourage the recognition of social security law as an independent academic subject, although some links with labour law are preserved. This recognition can be observed in the universities.

1.1.2   ECONOMIC AND SOCIAL CONTEXT

The Netherlands is a small country with a population of 14.3 million people. Population density is among the highest in the world. The establishment of the European Community has given a new dimension to the Netherlands' function as an economic link. Easy access from the North Sea has made the delta of the Rhine, Maas and Schelde the gateway to Europe and, as a result, a major centre of economic activity. A striking feature of this development is that the area's transit functions and related service activities have not been the only sectors to grow in importance: the delta has also become a favourite location for international organizations.

As a result the Dutch economy has experienced an almost uninterrupted expansion since World War II, with real national income more than doubling in the period from 1961 to 1982. Following the first oil crisis, however, the pace of the economy slowed down noticeably. The second oil crisis, in 1979, led to an actual stagnation at the beginning of the 1980s, from which there has now been a recovery. The economically active population is about 40.5 per cent of the total population. The main reason for this low percentage is the poor supply of, and demand for, women in the labour market. Traditionally, married women were expected to stay at home and care for their children. In recent years the number of economically active women has been increasing significantly, but this increase has occurred mainly in part-time jobs.

The working population is distributed between different sectors of the economy: 5.1 per cent is engaged in agriculture, 27.8 per cent in industry and 67.1 per cent in services.

1.2   SOURCES

1.2.1   INTERNATIONAL STANDARDS

In recent years, the courts have developed a tendency to apply international standards. This is particularly true in the field of social security, where reference has been made to United Nations conventions. Judges have extended existing rights, applying them to groups other than those explicitly provided for in legislation (for example, by extending widows' pensions to widowers), and prohibiting discrimination on grounds other than those explicitly provided for in legislation (for example, marital status).

This development was made possible by art. 93 of the Constitution which declares that any appropriate (in terms of its contents) provision in a treaty may be directly applied. Judges are thus increasingly prepared to apply treaty provisions, and in doing so to overrule conflicting national legislation.

1.2.1.1   Human rights

United Nations

The Netherlands has ratified the following United Nations legal instruments: the International Convention on the Elimination of All Forms of Racial Discrimination of 1965 was ratified in 1971;[1] the International Covenant on Economic, Social and Cultural Rights, and the International Covenant on Civil and Political Rights, both of 1966, were ratified in 1978;[2] and the Convention on the Elimination of All Forms of Discrimination against Women was ratified in 1991.[3]

International Labour Organization

The principle of equal treatment is one of the fundamental principles of the International Labour Organization (ILO); it was included in the Declaration of Philadelphia and in the ILO Constitution, 1949:

> All human beings, irrespective of race, creed or sex, have the right both to pursue their material well-being and their spiritual development in conditions of freedom and dignity, of economic security and equal opportunity.

---

[1]   Act of 18 February 1971, Stb 1971, 76.
[2]   Act of 24 November 1978, Stb 1978, 624.
[3]   Act of 3 July 1991, Stb 1991, 355.

The principle of non-discrimination has been repeated in a number of conventions and recommendations, for instance in the Discrimination (Employment and Occupation) Convention 1958 (No 111), the Social Policy (Basic Aims and Standards) Convention 1962 (No 117) and the Human Resources Development Convention 1975 (No 142), as well as in the Human Resources Development Recommendation 1975 (No 150).

The ILO dedicated the Equal Remuneration Convention 1951 (No 100)[1] to the fight against unequal treatment of men and women. The convention seeks to promote and, in so far as it is consistent with the methods in operation for determining rates of remuneration, to ensure that the principle of equal remuneration for men and women workers for work of equal value is applied to all workers (art. 2). Moreover, measures have to be taken to promote an objective appraisal of jobs on the basis of the work to be performed (art. 3). In the following years a number of conventions were adopted concerning discrimination in general in employment and social security, including the Workers with Family Responsibilities Convention 1981 (No 156).[2]

It is not clear whether, in the Netherlands, ILO conventions have direct effect in law,[3] although one writer has argued that a convention has direct effect once it has been ratified.[4] Details of the ratification of ILO conventions are noted at §7.2 below.

Council of Europe

The principle of equal treatment has been embodied in the European Convention for the Protection of Human Rights and Fundamental Freedoms, notably in art. 14. This provision states that 'the enjoyment of the rights and freedoms set forth in this Convention shall be secured without discrimination on any ground such as sex'. However, equal pay and equal treatment in employment are not mentioned among the rights and freedoms of this Convention.

The right to equal pay for men and women is laid down in art. 4(3) of the European Social Charter, 1961, which provides that 'the Contracting Parties undertake ... to recognize the right of men and women workers to equal pay for work of equal value'.[5]

It used to be generally accepted in the Netherlands that the provisions of the European Social Charter could not be relied upon by citizens before a

---

1   Trb 1952, 45.
2   Trb 1982, 101.
3   HR, 23 November 1984, NJ 1985, 604 mn Alkema.
4   A.T.J.M. JACOBS, *De rechtstreekse werking van internationale normer en het sociaal recht*, Alphen aan den Rijn, 1985.
5   See also the preamble to the Charter.

national court, possibly with the exception of cases in which the prohibition of discrimination was in question. However, in a number of cases direct effect has been implied for certain provisions of the European Social Charter, notably in the case of strikes.[1] There are no reported cases where the provisions concerning equal pay or equal treatment of men and women under the Charter have been invoked before a national court.

1.2.1.2 Treaties on special questions

In relation to night work, the Netherlands has withdrawn from ILO Convention No 89 so that a ban on night work could be lifted.

1.2.2 EUROPEAN COMMUNITY LAW

1.2.2.1 Direct effect of Community law

The attitude of the European Court of Justice (ECJ) concerning direct effect of Directives has been summarized by Timmermans as indicating that 'in order to be directly effective, a provision may not leave real discretionary powers to an implementing authority'.[2]

There has been no reported case in a Dutch court where one party relied on a provision in a Directive concerning discrimination against a private employer. It has been accepted, however, that in the application of national law, notably concerning the provisions of an Act which has been passed especially for the application of a Directive, the national courts have to interpret national law in the light of the words and the aims of the Directive. This was the case, for instance, in the *Dekker* case.[3] No case has been taken to the national courts invoking Directive 75/117/EEC concerning equal pay. In 1980 a litigant invoked Directive 76/207/EEC in a case against the Government in its capacity as employer before the *Ambtenarengerecht* (Civil Servants' Tribunal) of Rotterdam.[4] At that time, no equal treatment legislation existed for civil servants. The judge accepted that there was direct effect in that case.

In a number of cases Directive 79/7/EEC concerning equal treatment in social security has been the issue in litigation, notably since 19 December 1984. On 3 June 1987 the *Raad van Beroep* (appeal tribunal) of Groningen[5]

---

1 HR, 30 May 1986, NJ 1988, 688.
2 C.W.A.T. TIMMERMANS, 'Directives: their Effect within the National Legal Systems', CMLR, Vol. 16, No 4, pp 539-540.
3 *Dekker/VJV*, HR 13 September 1991, NJ 1992, 225; case taken to ECJ as *Dekker* v. *Stichting Vormingscentrum voor Jong Volwassenen*, Case C-177/88, [1990] ECR I-3941 (ECJ).
4 AG, Rotterdam, 18 February 1980, AB 1981, p. 164.
5 *NJCM-Bulletin* 12-5 (1987), Prg 1987, p. 337, No 2697.

and on 29 December 1987 the *Raad van Beroep* of Amsterdam[1] examined national social security rules in the light of the Directive, notably in the light of art. 4.[2] On 23 June 1992 the *Centrale Raad van Beroep* (Central Council for Appeals) held that the imposition of a threshold in the Act dealing with disability was indirectly discriminatory and in contravention of the Directive.[3]

1.2.2.2　Retrospective implementation

There has not been any retrospective implementation of EC law concerning equal treatment of men and women.

1.2.3　CONSTITUTIONAL LAW

Since 1983 art. 1 of the Netherlands Constitution contains a prohibition of discrimination. This provision is a successor to the former art. 4 of the 1979 Constitution, which provided for equal treatment for all who found themselves on the territory of the Kingdom. The equality rule is addressed both to the authorities in their relationship with the citizens, and to the citizens in their relations with each other. The general consensus of opinion is that art. 1 of the Constitution is one of the provisions which have or may have horizontal effect.[4] Under art. 120 of the Constitution the courts cannot test whether Acts are in conformity with the Constitution. A problem in the application of this rule, however, is that the meaning of the provision is not so sharply defined that a specific standard is given for the acts of the authorities with regard to the citizens and of the citizens with regard to each other.

Article 1 of the Constitution provides that equal cases should be treated equally, but there is no suggestion what form the treatment should take. The provision does, however, make clear that the use of criteria such as religion, race, sex, and so forth as yardsticks for decisions is not permitted. Moreover, it is not clear which factors are relevant in determining that two cases are equal, so that they have to be treated equally. There is also the question as to the extent that unequal cases may be treated unequally.

It follows from this that art. 1 of the Constitution does not sufficiently explain its meaning, and is more an aspirational than a concrete rule of conduct.

1　RSV 1988, 173.
2　See also *Centrale Raad van Beroep* (Central Council for Appeals), 19 April 1990, *Rechtspraak Nemesis*, 1990, p. 103, and 6 June 1991, RSV 1992, p. 75.
3　*NJCM-Bulletin*, 1993, p. 292.
4　See I.P. ASSCHER-VONK, *Toegang tot de Dienstbetrekking*, Alphen aan den Rijn, 1989, p. 206, for an overview of the opinions on this point.

1.2.4   LEGISLATION

1.2.4.1   Prior legislation

Before 1 July 1989, when an amendment of the Equal Treatment Act (*Wet Gelijke Behandeling*) was passed, equal pay for men and women was regulated in a separate piece of legislation, the Equal Pay Act (*Wet Gelijk Loon voor Vrouwen en Mannen*). The contents of this Act were for the most part consolidated within the Equal Treatment Act, which is now in force.

Equal pay and equal treatment for civil servants, now also embodied in the Equal Treatment Act, were separately provided for in the Equal Treatment Act (Civil Servants) of 1980. Finally, special legislation was enacted to prohibit the dismissal of married female teachers.[1]

1.2.4.2   Present legislation

Equal treatment of men and women employed under a contract of employment, whether in relation to pay or other conditions, is laid down in art. 1637ij of the Civil Code (*Burgerlijk Wetboek*). Equal pay and conditions of employment for other workers (civil servants and persons working for another) are provided for in the Equal Treatment Act, as are rules about equal treatment in recruitment to the liberal professions.

The Works Council Act (*Wet op de Ondernemingsraden*) of 1971 also contains a provision concerning equal treatment. Article 28(3) puts an obligation on works councils to be on their guard against discrimination in the undertaking, especially unequal treatment of men and women.

---

[1]   Act on Equal Treatment in case of Dismissal (*Wet Gelijke Behandeling in geval van beëindiging van de Dienstbetrekking*), Stb 1979, 278.

2.   BASIC CONCEPTS

2.1   EQUALITY AND DISCRIMINATION

The concepts of equality and discrimination were discussed in general terms on the occasion of the amendment of the Constitution in 1983. The relevant literature stresses the importance of the equality and non-discrimination clause in the Constitution.[1] It means in the first place that although citizens may be different, they have to be treated equally. In applying the equality principle the question arises as to the circumstances in which differences may lead to different treatment. The answer to that question is often a political or ethical one.

Discrimination is treatment of another person in a way that shows that in certain respects she or he is considered inferior.[2] One author has summed up the discussion about the meaning of art. 1 of the Constitution as follows:

> The equality principle implies that equal cases should be treated equally and unequal cases unequally, according to the degree of their inequality.[3]

The provision in the Constitution which provides for equal treatment and prohibits discrimination is an important one. It states that all residents of the Netherlands are entitled to protection of their person and goods, and are equal before the law and to be treated equally in equal cases.[4]

The concepts of equality and discrimination are, however, considered to be problematic. As one writer has put it:

> The provision knocks on an open door by stating that equal cases should be treated equally. However, the problem is ... not so much that equal cases are to be treated equally, but that (seemingly) unequal cases (seemingly) unequally.[5]

While the Parliamentary discussions about the revision of the Constitution were proceeding, the Government did not seem able to provide a definition of discrimination. The Minister replied to a number of such questions in Parliament as follows:

---

[1]   C.W. VAN DER POT-DONNER, *Handboek van het Nederlands Staatsrecht*, Zwolle, 1989.

[2]   TK, 1976-1977, p. 2150 *et seq.*

[3]   L.F.M. BESSELINK, in M. DE LANGEN *et al.*, *Kinderen en recht*, Deventer/Arnhem, 1989.

[4]   C.W. VAN DER POT-DONNER, *Handboek van het Nederlandse Staatsrecht*, Zwolle, 1989, p. 261.

[5]   C.A.J.M. KORTMANN, *De Grondwetscherzieningen 1983 en 1987*, Deventer, 1987, p. 62.

With discrimination it is like what St Augustine felt when asked for a definition of time: 'when I am asked I don't know, when I am not asked I know exactly'.[1]

Later the Government gave this definition:

The meaning of the ban on discrimination is the prohibition of any distinction based on qualities or characteristics of persons, which are in fairness not relevant to the setting of claims and duties in a certain field of society ... . This will mean that the prohibition of discrimination will be applicable only in relation to certain characteristics and qualities of persons. What characteristics and qualities these will be is to be determined by the social reality.[2]

2.2   DIRECT DISCRIMINATION

The concept of direct discrimination has met with few problems in Dutch literature and legal practice. A definition had been given in the 1978-1979 parliamentary documents of the Equal Treatment Act:[3] 'direct discrimination means a direct connection with a certain person's sex'. This did not leave much room for ambiguity, unlike the more difficult concept of indirect discrimination.

2.2.1   DEFINITION

Neither art. 1637ij of the Civil Code, nor the Equal Treatment Act, includes a definition of direct discrimination. Paragraph 5 of art. 1637ij of the Civil Code, and the identical provision in art. 1 of the Equal Treatment Act, state only that discrimination on the grounds of pregnancy, confinement and maternity is included in the concept of direct discrimination. The parliamentary documents[4] relating to the amendment of the Equal Treatment Act of 1 July 1989 repeat the statement already made in the parliamentary documents of 1978-1979 relating to the Equal Treatment Act as it read before 1 July 1989. That statement is that 'direct discrimination is discrimination which is directly related to a person's sex'. For the meaning of direct discrimination, therefore, the sources of literature and case law, both that of the Equal Treatment Committee (*Commissie Gelijke Behandeling van Mannen en Vrouwen*) and of the courts, have to be consulted.

2.2.1.1   Reason

Whether discrimination is intentional or unintentional does not make any difference to the question of whether there has been direct

---

1   TK, 1976-1977, p. 2150.
2   TK 1981-1982, 16 905-16, No 5, p. 16.
3   TK 15 400, 1-4, p. 10.
4   TK 19 908.

discrimination. The fact that the employer is not to blame does not reduce the potential claim for damages based on direct discrimination.[1]

2.2.1.2 Detriment

In some cases employers have argued that there was no direct discrimination because the discrimination was not detrimental to women. In *Beets-Proper/van Lanschot*,[2] for example, the employer argued that the different treatment was intended to protect women. This argument was rejected by the Equal Treatment Committee. In another case,[3] the employer recruited mostly men for the job of meter inspector, and he defended this with arguments based on safety: he stated that female meter inspectors would encounter more problems and would be molested. The Equal Treatment Committee rejected this argument, stating that the prohibition of discrimination in recruitment does not allow the protection of women as an exception.

2.2.1.3 Comparator

Article 1637ij of the Civil Code, which provides for equal treatment in pay and other conditions of employment, is addressed to the employer. This means that only a comparison of a man and a woman who are both employed by the same employer is possible.[4] One author argues that this seems reasonable and sufficient.[5] Every employer has to comply with the same rule, so a comparison between two persons employed by different employers could not lead to another or better result than a comparison between two employees of the same employer. This reasoning is however, as the same writer points out, only partially conclusive. Cross-industry comparisons would enable more cases to be decided where the jobs are directly or nearly comparable. Also, cross-industry comparisons would make comparisons possible for jobs which are predominantly single sex. The author argues therefore that it would be important to have as broad a frame of reference as possible. In the amendment to the Equal Treatment Act of 1989 no change in that context was introduced.

In the Equal Pay Act, the previous rule was that a person could compare herself or himself with a person of the other sex within the employer's

---

1   *Dekker* v. *Stichting Vormingscentrum voor Jong Volwassenen*, Case C-177/88, [1990] ECR 3941, NJ 1992, 224 (ECJ). See I.P. ASSCHER-VONK, 'Gevolgen van het Dekker-arrest voor de sanctionering van gelijke behandelingsregels', SMA 1993, p. 186 *et seq*; see also I.P. ASSCHER-VONK, 'Transformation of Civil Law Sanctions' in M. VERWILGHEN (Ed.), *Access to Equality between Men and Women*, Louvain-la-Neuve, 1993.

2   *Beets-Proper/van Lanschot*, HR 2 November 1984, NJ 1987, 349, and 21 November 1986, NJ 1987, 351.

3   Equal Treatment Committee, 3 April 1985; see A.M. GERRITSEN, *Rechtspraak gelijke behandeling*, p. 334.

4   TK 15 400, 6, p. 15.

5   J.J. VAN DER WEELE, *Wet Gelijke Behandeling van Mannen en Vrouwen*, Deventer, 1983, p. 25.

enterprise or, if need be, in an enterprise in the same sector of industry. That fairly broad possibility of comparison was narrowed down when the Equal Treatment Act was amended in 1989 and the equal pay rule was incorporated into that Act. The equal pay rule is now laid down in art. 1637ij(1) of the Civil Code, and for civil servants in art. 1a of the Equal Treatment Act. The scope for comparison has been restricted to the enterprise of the employer.

The legislature seems not to have been aware of the meaning of this change. The parliamentary documents state that the equal pay rule has been left unchanged.[1] The limiting of the possibilities for comparison has been defended by the argument that the broader possibilities of the Equal Pay Act were hardly ever used. This argument does not seem conclusive in the light of the fact that not much use has been made of the possibilities of the Equal Pay Act, which may be attributed to factors such as fear of losing one's job. A special problem which was raised in 1983 is the question whether discrimination on the ground of discriminatory criteria, such as pregnancy, between a woman and a woman (or between a man and a man) does in fact amount to breach of the equal treatment rule.[2] It is suggested that that is not the case, since the Equal Treatment Act forbids discrimination between men and women, and not between women themselves. The question was put to the ECJ in the *Dekker* case[3] by the *Hoge Raad* (Supreme Court). The ECJ held that the fact that there are no male applicants for a post does not change the directly discriminatory nature of the refusal; if a decision is directly connected with a person's sex it does not matter that there are no applicants of the other sex.[4]

2.2.2 EXTENDED DEFINITION

The definition of direct discrimination has been extended by the Equal Treatment Committee. In its annual report for 1984 the Committee stated that there is direct discrimination in cases where there is a reference to features that are necessarily connected with a particular sex.

Extended definitions have been used in legal commentaries. One author has described direct discrimination as overt, clearly traceable discrimination,[5] whereby a division between men and women is brought about, resulting in a different treatment of persons of a particular sex. The author continued by arguing that direct discrimination can be committed not only by choosing sex as a criterion, but also by reference to qualities or features which are necessarily connected with a certain sex, such as the possibility of pregnancy

---

1 TK 19 908, 3, p. 5.
2 J.J. VAN DER WEELE, *Wet Gelijke Behandeling van Mannen en Vrouwen*, Deventer, 1983, pp 60-61.
3 HR, 24 June 1988, NJ 1989, 1002.
4 *Dekker* v. *Stichting Vormingscentrum voor Jong Volwassenen*, Case C-177/88, [1990] ECR 3941, NJ 1992, p. 224 (ECJ).
5 W.J.P.M. FASE, *Gelijke behandeling van vrouw en man in de sociale zekerheid*, Deventer, 1986, p. 48.

and maternity, or with a legal position which is only attributed to one of the sexes, such as conscription for compulsory military service or the position of head of household.[1]

2.2.2.1 Marital status

In the definitions of direct discrimination in Dutch law, marital status and family status do not feature as criteria by which the definition has been extended.

2.2.2.2 Family status

See §2.2.2.1 above.

2.2.2.3 Pregnancy

As pointed out above, an extension of the definition of direct discrimination to cover pregnancy, confinement and maternity has been made both in legal literature and in the Equal Treatment Committee's case law.

In the Committee's case law any reference to pregnancy has been held to amount to direct discrimination and, unless there is a case of a permitted exception, to a breach of the equal treatment rule.[2] The courts have however allowed objective justifications to be put forward in cases where a reference to pregnancy had been made, thus implicitly considering a reference to pregnancy as indirect discrimination. In 1989, on the occasion of the amendment of the Equal Treatment Act, the legal definition of direct discrimination in art. 1637ij(5) and art. 1 of the Equal Treatment Act was extended so that it now contains a reference to pregnancy. No attention was given to a reference to legal status, such as the status of conscription, an extension which was not only mentioned in legal literature but was also used by the Equal Treatment Committee.[3]

2.2.2.4 Sexual harassment

Sexual harassment has not yet been accepted as a form of direct discrimination. Whether the issue of sexual harassment is relevant to equal treatment is a subject of continuing discussion.

---

[1] It should be noted that in Dutch law the head of household concept has disappeared and has been replaced by the breadwinner concept, which does not directly discriminate but may amount to indirect discrimination.

[2] Equal Treatment Committee, Annual Report, 1984, p. 40.

[3] Equal Treatment Committee, 2 April 1984 and 18 December 1984; A.M. GERRITSEN, *Rechtspraak gelijke behandeling m/v*, Leiden, 1987, pp 369 and 392.

2.2.2.5   Physical attributes

A reference to physical attributes may amount to direct discrimination if it concerns attributes which are necessarily connected with a particular sex. Examples, e.g. a soprano voice for the singer of a certain part, have been put forward as instances in which a person's sex is a determining factor.[1] In these cases there is an exception to the equal treatment rule. Since July 1989 there has been a list of attributes which may cause a person's sex to be a determining factor (see §4.2.2 below).

2.2.2.6   Dress codes

Dress codes have been the issue in cases where they were part of the conditions of employment (see §4.8 below). In a case where the dress regulations for aircraft attendants prescribed that men had to wear caps under certain circumstances, while women were free to choose whether or not they wore their hats under the same circumstances, this was held to amount to direct discrimination.[2] A dress code which stated that male hospital personnel had to wear a certain coat and jacket, while female personnel had to wear a dress, was considered directly discriminatory, because women had to have the choice of wearing trouser suits.[3]

2.2.2.7   Military service

In Dutch legal literature[4] and in the Equal Treatment Committee's case law,[5] a reference to compulsory military service is considered to be direct discrimination. The argument has been put forward that military service is a reference to a legal status which affects persons of one sex only. The Equal Treatment Committee has argued that a reference to military service means that a large number of candidates are excluded, including in any case all women.[6] A reference to the status of conscientious objector also amounts to direct discrimination because, as the Equal Treatment Committee has pointed out, 'no conscientious objector is of the female sex'.

---

1   TK 15 400, 1-4, p. 11.
2   Equal Treatment Committee, 28 September 1987.
3   Equal Treatment Committee for Civil Servants, 28 September 1987.
4   W.J.P.M. FASE (ed.), *Gelijke behandeling van vrouw en man in de sociale zekerheid*, Deventer, 1986, p. 48.
5   See A.M. GERRITSEN, *Rechtspraak gelijke behandeling m/v*, Leiden, 1987 (GERRITSEN I), p. 51.
6   See literature and case law mentioned by A.M. GERRITSEN, *op. cit.*, p. 56, notes 75 and 76.

2.3 INDIRECT DISCRIMINATION

2.3.1 DEFINITION

Following the amendments of 1989 and 1994, Article 1637ij(5) of the Civil Code contains the following definition of indirect discrimination:

> Indirect discrimination means a distinction on the ground of qualities other than sex, for instance marital status or family circumstances, which results in discrimination on the ground of sex. The prohibition of distinctions imposed by the first paragraph of this article does not apply to distinctions which are objectively justified.

Articles 1 and 6 of the Equal Treatment Act contain a similar definition.

In the parliamentary documents relating to the 1989 amendment some explanation is given, notably with reference to the case law of the ECJ, which is even quoted *verbatim*. The documents state:

> The definition is connected with the case law of the European Court of Justice of the European Communities. Preference is given to the approach of the Court over the wording formulated by the European Parliament . (...) It is not considered desirable to provide further refinement or criteria in the Act.[1]

The documents continue later:

> The term 'objective justification' means that, if the use of a certain criterion is detrimental to persons of one sex, it is necessary that the use of the criterion can be explained by factors which are objectively justified and are not related to discrimination on the grounds of sex. There should also be a reasonable relationship between the objective pursued and the measures employed to achieve that objective.

> In the *Bilka/Weber* case of 13 May 1986 the European Court of Justice further pursued the yardstick to be used when defining indirect discrimination. The Court left the judgment about the facts and whether the arguments the employer brought forward were objectively justified and were not related to sex discrimination to the national courts. When making that judgment however, the Court should evaluate whether 'the measures chosen correspond to a real need on the part of the undertaking, are appropriate with a view to achieving the objectives pursued and are necessary to that end'. Both elements link closely with the remarks the Emancipation Council made in this respect.[2]

2.3.2 SUSPECT CRITERIA

Breadwinner

The breadwinner concept has been a suspect criterion from the inception of the equal treatment legislation, and is mentioned as such in the preparatory papers to the Equal Treatment Act of 1980. The argument that the concept of breadwinner is a suspect criterion has been put forward as follows:

---

[1]   TK 19 908, 5b, p. 2.
[2]   TK 19 908, 6, p. 12.

The idea that a couple can decide for themselves who is to take up the role of breadwinner does not hold up. ... It is clear that a lot has to change in the field of education, promotion possibilities, and so forth, before one can say that men and women have equal earning capacity. More generally, there is ... no question of free choice as long as the circumstances under which the choices in our society have to be made are so different for men and women. With reference to the notion that breadwinners should have preference in the distribution of work, we will remark in the first place that the right to work should be considered individually and not by family.[1]

In the case law of the Equal Treatment Committee, a reference to the concept of breadwinner is considered to amount to a likelihood of indirect discrimination. Where, however, it is not clear that the reference is detrimental to women, there is no indirect discrimination.[2]

Whether or not the breadwinner concept should be allowed to play a role in social security benefits is a more difficult question. Now that the question as to whether breadwinner allowances in the General Disability Act (*Algemene Arbeidsongeschiktheidswet*) were in conformity with Directive 79/7/EEC has been answered in the negative in the decision in *Teuling-Worms*,[3] the question arises as to whether allowances for spouses in the State pension scheme are acceptable.

Full-time/part-time work

The status of full-time and part-time worker has featured in recent years as a suspect criterion in the Equal Treatment Committee's case law.[4] In its opinion of 1986 the Committee argued as follows:

Since part-time workers — as is generally known — are mainly women, the use of the 'part-time' criterion, or a criterion 'with special reference to part-timers' does create a suspicion of indirect discrimination.[5]

The Equal Treatment Committee for Civil Servants argued that 'based on social reality it is to be considered a fact that within the Civil Service and within education part-time workers are mainly women'.[6] The *Gerechtshof* (Regional Court) of The Hague, in its judgment of 21 February 1986,[7] also considered reference to part-time work to amount to indirect discrimination in principle, although in that case an objective justification for the indirect discrimination was accepted.

---

[1]   TK 15 400, 6, pp 6 and 7.
[2]   Equal Treatment Committee, 18 November 1982, GERRITSEN I, *op.cit.,* No 88.
[3]   29 November 1988, RvB Amsterdam, RSV 1988, 173.
[4]   STICHTING VAN DE ARBEID, *Advies arbeidsvoorwaarden en wetgeving gelijke behandeling,* 31 October 1987.
[5]   Equal Treatment Committee, 7 July 1986, GERRITSEN I, *op. cit.,* No 30.
[6]   Equal Treatment Committee for Civil Servants, August 1983, GERRITSEN I, *op. cit.,* No 90.
[7]   GERRITSEN I, p. 28.

The *Buitengewoon Besluit Arbeidsverhoudingen* (BBA: Labour Relations Decree), which prohibits the dismissal of an employee without the prior consent of the Director of the Regional Labour Office (*Gewestelijk Arbeidsbureau*), excludes part-time household employees from its scope. The justification for this exclusion was:
(a) the administrative burden which would arise if such employees were included in the scope of the BBA;
(b) the interference with the privacy of those concerned which would be the consequence of an effective protection against dismissal; and
(c) the fact that the exclusion is analogous to that of social security law.[1]

This justification could be considered inadequate.[2] The same exclusion that existed in the BBA was included in various social security Acts, notably the legislation which is applicable to employed persons. In that area, the justification was similar, and perhaps insufficient.[3] Similarly, the exclusion of part-time household employees in the BBA is to be considered to contravene Directive 76/207/EEC.

Working hours

Hours of work have not figured as suspect criteria in Dutch legal literature and case law.

Marital status/Family status

Marital or family status have consistently been considered (in the same way as the concept of breadwinner and for the same reasons) as suspect criteria.

Pregnancy

A reference to pregnancy is now, as has been shown above, seen as direct discrimination. In the case law of the Equal Treatment Committee, a reference to pregnancy was considered direct discrimination before the change in the law took place. A reference to circumstances connected with the pregnancy, such as for instance the fact that the woman would be on leave for a considerable time, was considered to amount to a suspicion of indirect discrimination, which could however be objectively justified. In case law a reference to the consequences of the pregnancy has more often than not been considered to be a reference to the pregnancy itself. In the parliamentary documents concerning the amendment of the Equal Treatment Act, where reference to pregnancy was labelled as direct discrimination, no

---

1 TK 19 810, p. 3.
2 See I.P. ASSCHER-VONK, 'Wijziging van het BBA', NJB 1987, p. 235.
3 See J. MANNOURY and I.P. ASSCHER-VONK, *Hoofdtrekken van de sociale verzekering*, Alphen aan den Rijn, 1987, p. 78.

attention was given to the question as to whether a reference to pregnancy-related circumstances may be direct or indirect discrimination.

Mobility requirement

The idea of a mobility requirement has not been explicitly raised. Comparable with mobility is the requirement that a person should be ready and able to work in different departments, including shifts. The question whether this requirement amounts or may amount to indirect discrimination was raised in the *van Dam* case.[1] The Equal Treatment Committee argued in that case that a mobility requirement may result in indirect discrimination. The Regional Court confirmed the ruling that there was a suspicion of indirect discrimination.

Strength

The requirement of strength has not arisen in Dutch law.

Safety

Safety was an issue in the case of a female meter inspector. The employer preferred to employ men for safety reasons. The Committee ruled that this was direct discrimination, and that exclusion based on the protection of women was not applicable.

Age limits

Age limits as possible indirectly discriminatory factors have not arisen in the case law of the Equal Treatment Committee or the courts. There are signs that the subject of age discrimination is receiving more attention in the Netherlands legal literature.[2]

Minimum height requirements

Minimum height requirements have been considered to be indirectly discriminatory, unless they correspond to a real need. In the leading case on this question a man, who did not meet the minimum height requirements for male police officers (for whom the minimum height was higher than for women), successfully appealed under the Equal Treatment Act.[3]

---

[1] *Gerechtshof* (Regional Court) 's-Hertogenbosch, 17 April 1984, NJ 1985, 202.
[2] See A.M. GERRITSEN, *Onderscheid naar leeftijd in het arbeidsrecht*, Deventer, 1994.
[3] *Rechtbank* (District Court) 's-Gravenhage, 22 June 1981, unreported.

Seniority

The application of seniority was considered to be contrary to the equal treatment principle by the Equal Treatment Committee in the *van Dam* case.[1] It is however also possible that in some cases a departure from the seniority rule may be detrimental to women and therefore may result in indirect discrimination.[2]

Preference for existing employees

Preference for existing employees has not arisen in case law as a criterion of indirect discrimination, although the matter has been raised in the relevant literature.[3] It is at any rate possible to argue that a preference for existing employees may amount to indirect discrimination, unless there is an objective justification.

2.3.3 DISPROPORTIONATE IMPACT

Statistical evidence and relevant pools

In principle, statistical evidence is accepted as a way of establishing *prima facie* evidence of indirect discrimination. There is no unanimity, however, about what the relevant pools are. There are a number of possible methods to determine these pools and some of these have been employed by the Equal Treatment Committee and the courts:

(1) In one case it was considered how many men, and how many women, were disadvantaged by a certain rule or criterion, and whether women formed the majority in the affected group.[4]
(2) In the same case the Regional Court, on appeal, considered whether more women than men were disadvantaged within the group out of which the new appointees were to be recruited.
(3) Another problem has been choosing which part of the population forms the relevant group. In a case decided on 17 March 1988 the Equal Treatment Committee counted all employees in the department of the enterprise in question.[5]
(4) In some cases the Equal Treatment Committee has also looked at the total workforce of the employer.[6]

---

1 Equal Treatment Committee, 7 May 1984, *Gerechtshof* (Regional Court) 's-Hertogenbosch, 17 April 1984.
2 Equal Treatment Committee, 23 January 1985.
3 I.P. ASSCHER-VONK, *Toegang tot de dienstbetrekking*, Alphen aan den Rijn, 1989, p. 199.
4 President *Rechtbank* (District Court) in the *Herstructurering Onderwijs Salariëring* (HOS) case, appealed in Hof 's-Gravenhage, 17 February 1988, NJ 1988, 919.
5 C.M. SJERPS, 'Tellen en tellen is twee', SMA 1985, p. 367: the author states that the choosing of the department as the relevant pool is logical.
6 Equal Treatment Committee, 9 April 1984 and 29 March 1985.

(5) It has also been argued that the situation in society as a whole is used as a basis for comparison. This happens in response to arguments such as: 'it is generally known that part-timers are mostly women'.[1]

Impact on the individual

This has not arisen in Dutch law.

2.3.4   OBJECTIVE JUSTIFICATION

In the information leaflet issued by the Equal Treatment Committee after the amendment of the Equal Treatment Act of 1 July 1989,[2] the 'real need' element of the objective justification was explained as follows: the objective should be reasonable (for instance, the proper functioning of the enterprise) and sufficiently important to be balanced against the equality principle. The same leaflet stated that it also had to be considered whether the regulation under consideration was *appropriate* and *necessary* for the objective pursued. In other words, the way in which an otherwise justifiable objective is pursued should be free of discrimination. That would not be the case when the objective could be achieved in another, less discriminating, way. There is little case law from the courts. The concept of objective justification has not been clarified.

2.4   VICTIMIZATION

Article 1637ij(6) of the Civil Code reads:

An employer's termination of an employment relationship where the worker has lodged a complaint, either judicially or extra-judicially, under the provisions of the first paragraph of this article, shall be null and void. The worker shall be entitled to claim that termination a nullity for a period of two months after he received notice, or for a period of two months after the employment relationship was terminated if the employer terminated it otherwise than by giving notice. Such nullity shall be claimed by means of a notification served on the employer. The employer shall not be liable for damages on account of his termination of the employment relationship referred to in the first sentence of this paragraph.

Article 1a of the Equal Treatment Act further reads:

(4) The competent authority may not terminate the employment of a person employed in the civil service because the person concerned has lodged a complaint, either judicially or extra-judicially, under the provisions of the first paragraph.

(5) The termination contrary to this law of an employment relationship of a person who is employed in the civil service on a Civil Code employment contract will not make the authority liable for damages. In that case the person concerned

---

[1] See C.H.S. EVENHUIS, *De Zykant van het gelijk*, Zwolle, 1991, p. 39.
[2] *Ministerie van Sociale Zaken en Werkgelegenheid*, The Hague, 1989.

shall be entitled to claim nullity within a period of two months after he received notice, or after the employment relationship was terminated if the competent authority has terminated it otherwise than by giving notice. Such nullity shall be claimed by means of a notice served on the employer.

Every claim of the person concerned in connection with the annulment of the termination under this paragraph becomes barred after a lapse of time of six months.

One may doubt whether these measures are sufficient. If these provisions are compared with art. 21 of the Works Council Act, which provides protection against reprisals for members, former members or candidates for the works council, two differences are notable. In the first place, art. 21 of the Works Council Act also offers protection for reprisals other than termination of the employment relationship in that it provides that the employer must ensure that 'members of the works council ... are not damaged in their position within the enterprise because of their membership of the works council'. In the second place, art. 21 of the Works Council Act provides for a time limit within which the former member of the works council cannot be dismissed in the usual way, whereas the Equal Treatment Act gives no time limit within which dismissal is presumed to be because of a complaint under the Equal Treatment Act.

3.   EQUAL PAY

3.1   PRINCIPLE

The equal pay rule is, since the Equal Treatment Act was amended on 1 July 1989, set out in art. 1637ij(1) of the Civil Code and art. 1a(1) of the Equal Treatment Act, elaborated in arts 7-11 of the Act. The principle in these provisions is adopted from the previous equal pay legislation. The principle in the previous legislation was that a female employee had a right to receive equal pay for work of 'nearly equal' value arising directly out of the contract of employment. To establish the nearly equal value of work the job had to be evaluated in a sound job classification scheme.[1] In the amended Equal Treatment Act, the principle is that pay is considered to be included in working conditions, and the equal pay rule is contained within the provision that the employer is prohibited from making a distinction between men and women in relation to working conditions.[2]

No changes of substance were intended in this amendment. It may be doubted, however, whether the provision in the amended legislation that 'an employer shall not make any distinction between men and women when entering into a contract of employment, providing training for a worker, determining his conditions of employment, deciding on his promotion or terminating his contract of employment' does provide for a claim against the employer in the same way as the previous provision did. For instance, a woman applicant does not enjoy an explicit claim against the employer under the new provision. Of course one could argue that the employer's obligation must produce as its counterpart the employee's claim; an explicit provision, however, would have been clearer.

3.2   EXCEPTIONS

The only exceptions permitted by law are the following:
(a) cases where a person's sex is a determining factor;
(b) cases involving the protection of women, particularly in the context of pregnancy and maternity;
(c) measures to promote equal opportunity for women by removing existing inequalities.

3.3   PERSONAL SCOPE

3.3.1   EMPLOYEES

The personal scope of the relevant law is limited to employees with a contract of employment, that is to say an agreement under which one party,

---

[1]   TK 13 031, 3, p. 7.
[2]   Cf. HR 24 April 1992, JAR 1992, 14 (*Bouma/KLM*).

the employee, undertakes to perform work in the service of the other party, the employer, at specified times in return for remuneration (art. 1637a of the Civil Code). Article 1b of the Equal Treatment Act provides that if an individual, body corporate or other authority lets a person perform work in its service in any way other than under a contract of employment or enlistment as a civil servant, art. 1637ij of the Civil Code applies. Article 1b of the Equal Treatment Act thus has a broad application covering all those working in service. However, all those workers who do not perform their task in the service of an employer remain outside the scope of the equal treatment legislation.

3.3.2   INDEPENDENT CONTRACTORS

For some independent contractors (the legislature had particularly in mind practitioners of the liberal professions) art. 2 of the Equal Treatment Act provides the same protection as art. 1637ij(1) of the Civil Code does for employees.

3.3.3   HOME WORKERS

Some home workers are employed on a contract of employment as described in art. 1637a of the Civil Code: in those cases art. 1637ij(1) applies. In other cases the position of the home worker does not fit with the description in art. 1637a of the Civil Code. The element of 'in service' in particular seems to be absent in a number of cases, since home workers are for instance usually free to choose their working hours and place of work, and do not receive instructions as to how the work has to be performed. These home workers do not fit into the scope of art. 1637ij of the Civil Code and are also excluded from the scope of the Equal Treatment Act.

3.3.4   PUBLIC SECTOR

Workers in the public sector are covered by the Equal Treatment Act, notably in art. 1a. This provision also covers military personnel.

3.3.5   DOMESTIC EMPLOYEES

Domestic employees are not excluded from the scope of art. 1637ij of the Civil Code, since they will normally be employed under a contract of employment.

3.3.6   NON-EMPLOYED POPULATION

The non-employed population is not covered by this legislation.

3.4   ACTIVITIES COVERED

Activities covered by art. 1637ij of the Civil Code and the Equal Treatment Act include those performed under a contract of employment, under an appointment as a civil servant or military officer, or in an employment relationship where a person is in the service of somebody else.[1]

3.5   DEFINITION OF REMUNERATION

3.5.1   ARTICLE 119 OF THE EEC TREATY

In Dutch legal literature it is accepted that the definition of 'pay' in art. 119 is broad: it includes the normal basic pay or minimum wages and all benefits in money or in kind which the employer pays the employee on account of the employment relationship. It is clear that reimbursement of expenses is included under art. 119 and is considered to be pay under the Equal Pay Act.[2]

3.5.2   FRINGE BENEFITS

Remuneration is the performance by the employer to which the employee is *entitled* by virtue of the contract of employment. Gratuities to which the employee is not actually entitled are not regarded as remuneration. In practice, difficulties sometimes arise about such extras (for instance, the payment for a '13th month' at the end of the year). If the employer is obliged to pay the extra it is considered to be remuneration, but if he is free to grant it or refuse it, it is not. The answer in any case is to be found in the construction of the contract in question.[3]

3.5.3   CONTRIBUTIONS BY EMPLOYER

These contributions are not part of remuneration.[4]

3.5.4   CONTRIBUTIONS BY EMPLOYEE

Since remuneration is defined as the performance of the contract of employment by the employer, contributions by the employee are not considered to be remuneration.

---

1   Article 1(b) of the Equal Treatment Act.
2   TK 13 031, 22.
3   H.L. BAKELS, The Netherlands, p. 45, in the *International Encyclopaedia of Labour Law and Industrial Relations*.
4   H.L. BAKELS, *Schets van het Nederlands Arbeidsrecht*, 1994, p. 61.

3.5.5 POST-CONTRIBUTION BENEFITS

Post-contribution benefits and pensions are not considered to be remuneration, indicating a possible conflict between Dutch law and art. 119 of the EEC Treaty.[1]

3.5.6 PENSIONS

See §3.5.5 above.

3.5.7 COLLECTIVE AGREEMENTS

Collective agreements are not specifically regulated in the context of equal pay.

3.6 COMPARATOR

3.6.1 SAME ESTABLISHMENT

The Equal Pay Act 1975 (now superseded) contained a provision that, if in the establishment where the employee worked no work of equal value was performed by an employee of the other sex, the comparison should be made with the wages which an employee of the other sex received for work of equal value or nearly equal value in a similar establishment in the same industry (art. 3 of the Equal Pay Act). A similar provision does not appear in art. 1637ij of the Civil Code, as it now reads, nor in the Equal Treatment Act as amended. This is explained in the parliamentary documents by the fact that the possibility of comparison with the pay of an employee in another enterprise in the same industry had not been used.[2] However, it must be borne in mind that the use of the Equal Pay Act had been minimal overall.

3.6.2 CONTEMPORANEOUS EMPLOYMENT

On the basis of the law as worded the possibility of comparison does not appear to be restricted to contemporaneous employment. There is, however, no case law confirming this. In the parliamentary documents relating to the Equal Pay Act the opposite position was taken. The Minister remarked that in his opinion it would not be possible to compare the job as performed by an employee with the job of an employee who was no longer employed. Any comparison using job classification systems made the observation of the job performance necessary.

---

[1]   W.J.P.M. FASE, SMA 1982.
[2]   TK 19 908, 3, p. 22.

3.6.3   HYPOTHETICAL MALE

Under the former Equal Pay Act the comparison with an actual employee of the other sex was necessary. The wording of art. 1637ij of the Civil Code (which now covers equal pay) seems to leave open the possibility of a comparison with a hypothetical male.

3.6.4   DIFFERENT ESTABLISHMENT

See §3.6.1 above.

3.6.5   CROSS-INDUSTRY COMPARISONS

The possibility of cross-industry comparisons was discussed and rejected in the parliamentary documents relating to the Equal Pay Act.[1] Since the possibilities of comparison have been narrowed down with the amendment of the Equal Treatment Act of 1 July 1989, the possibility of cross-industry comparisons is now reduced.

3.7   WOMAN DOES SAME WORK AS MAN

The Equal Pay Act 1975, the relevant provisions of which are unchanged in the Equal Treatment Act, as amended, already contained the requirement that the comparison should be made with the wages which a person of the other sex usually received for work of equal value, or if there was none, work of nearly equal value. In the parliamentary documents it was noted that the question as to what is work of equal value had to be answered by applying sound systems of job evaluation. The concept 'work of nearly equal value' had been introduced to promote the practical applicability of the law. When jobs are compared, it is not always possible to find jobs of exactly equal value, for instance with the same rating. On the other hand, jobs with only a small difference in rating may be found which are, in spite of the small difference in rating, put in the same earning-class.[2]

3.8   EQUAL VALUE

3.8.1   JOB EVALUATION

See §3.8.2 below.

3.8.2   JOB CLASSIFICATION

Job evaluation plays a central role in the assessment of the work. Article 8 of the Equal Treatment Act provides that:

---

[1]   TK 13 031, 3, p. 8.
[2]   TK 13 031, 5-6 , p. 6.

For the purposes of article 7 work shall be assessed in accordance with a reliable system of job evaluation; to this end recourse shall be had as far as possible to the system customary in the undertaking where the worker concerned is employed. In the absence of such a system, the work shall be fairly assessed in the light of the available information.

Job evaluation systems have become widely used in the Netherlands since World War II.

Article 8 of the Equal Treatment Act provides that the job evaluation system has to be reliable. If no job evaluation system, or a faulty one, is used in an undertaking, the assessment of the work has to be made in good faith. The parliamentary documents for the Act state that if no job evaluation system or a faulty one is used, a more appropriate system must be applied.[1] What happens in practice is that the officers of the *Loontechnische Dienst* (LTD: Service for technical wage matters)[2] when making an enquiry assess the complainant's job and the job of the person she or he is comparing herself or himself with using the undertaking's or a widely used system of job evaluation. The LTD however does as a rule not conduct a job evaluation if from interviews with the employer and the employee it is apparent that they agree about the equal value of the jobs.[3]

The application of a job evaluation system is, however, not considered to amount to a guarantee of non-discriminatory practices. When a job evaluation system is used in an enterprise, there may be unequal pay because the system is applied in a discriminatory way.

There has also been a discussion concerning the extent to which a job evaluation system can necessarily be considered to be reliable, especially when considering that a job evaluation system may contain discriminatory elements. This issue has been addressed both in literature[4] and in political debate.[5]

3.8.2.1/2 Factors/Weighting

Job evaluation systems may be found discriminatory for different reasons. One of them is the choice of factors; the question which arises is whether factors which are characteristic in traditionally female jobs are given

---

[1] TK 13 031, 3, p. 7.

[2] These are appointed pursuant to art. 18 of the General Equal Treatment Act to assist the Equal Treatment Committee in its enquiries.

[3] A. Ph. JASPERS and M.T.C. VAN KLEINWEE, *Gelijke behandeling; je goed recht?* Ministerie van Sociale Zaken en Werkgelegenheid (Ministry of Social Affairs and Employment), 1985.

[4] L. BOELENS and A. VELDMAN, *Gelijkwaardige arbeid, gelijk gewaardeerd,* Utrecht, 1993.

[5] TK 19 908, 5, pp 39, 40, and 19 908, 6, pp 13, 37.

a sufficient value. The relative weighting of factors is also important. At the request of Parliament, the Minister for Social Affairs and Employment commissioned the LTD to examine job evaluation systems. The report was issued in 1988,[1] and concluded that it did not appear that women were systematically disadvantaged by the application of job evaluation systems.

It was also promised at an earlier stage that an investigation would be carried out into the *de facto* discrimination within job evaluation systems themselves. However, preliminary investigations indicated that an investigation of job evaluation systems themselves would not lead to unambiguous findings about the discriminatory character of these systems. The Minister for Social Affairs and Employment therefore decided not to proceed with this investigation.[2]

3.8.3   HIGHER VALUE

In opinions of 7 August and 23 August 1988 the Equal Treatment Committee ruled in a case where the woman's job had higher value, but the woman was paid less than the man with whom she was compared.[3] The Committee ruled that the woman was entitled to at least the same pay as the man.

3.8.4   PROPORTIONATE PAY

There is no relevant law in the Netherlands on this point.

3.9   LEGITIMATE REASON FOR PAY DIFFERENTIAL

In the parliamentary documents relating to the Equal Pay Act 1975 it was pointed out that the term 'equal pay' does not mean an identical total sum. The wages actually paid to a man and a woman for work of equal value may differ, for instance because the man did more overtime, or because there was a difference in seniority. Equal pay merely requires that the different factors which determine the pay level do not discriminate between men and women.[4]

Case law does not seem consistent. The *Hoge Raad* (Supreme Court) has held that 'historical reasons' are not legitimate factors for a pay differential between men and women.[5] The *Kantonrechter* (Cantonal Judge)

---

1   *Loontechnische Dienst: Toepassing van bedrijfstakgebonden functiewaarderings-regelingen in Nederland,* Ministerie van Sociale Zaken en Werkgelegenheid, September 1988.
2   *Toepassing van bedrijfstakgebonden functiewaarderingsregelingen in Nederland,* p. 2.
3   GERRITSEN II, p. 9, No 3.
4   TK 13 031, 3, p. 8.
5   HR, 13 November 1987, NJ 1989, 698.

of Amsterdam on the other hand[1] has ruled that a pay difference caused by a temporary measure was legitimate. In that case, female pursers were employed from 1977, from which date a new wages regulation came into force. Pursers in service from 1977, all male, received more salary than pursers employed from 1977 (male and female). The *Hoge Raad* held that the difference amounted to indirect discrimination.[2]

3.9.1   MATERIAL DIFFERENCE

Material differences which can account for legitimate reasons for pay differential may include:

(a) working conditions for persons posted abroad (for example, Turks posted in Holland) are more onerous than for persons working in their own countries;[3]
(b) the man with whom the woman compares herself works independently and represents continuity in the enterprise;[4]
(c) there are differences in performance.[5]

3.9.2   ECONOMIC BENEFITS/MARKET FORCES

The circumstances in which market forces have influenced remuneration include the determination of a person's pay on the basis of the pay received in a former job. This practice can obviously be detrimental to women. The *Hoge Raad*[6] has ruled that there is no objective justification for the use of the this criterion, unless work experience plays a role. More particularly, the argument that a person's pay should not decrease is not an objective justification in the *Hoge Raad*'s view.

The Equal Treatment Committee has given its opinion in this matter on a number of occasions, and has indicated that a cautious approach is called for which must be based on a sound policy.[7] In its annual report for 1988-1989, the Equal Treatment Committee made a few general remarks concerning the matter. The Committee stated that since market value or bargaining power were criteria which were detrimental for women, there was a suspicion of indirect discrimination in cases where any such criterion was

---

1   *Kantonrechter* Amsterdam, 16 March 1989, GERRITSEN II, p. 4; *NJCM-Bulletin* 1989, p. 928.
2   HR, 24 April 1992, JAR 1992, 14 (*Bouma/KLM*).
3   Equal Treatment Committee, 23 February 1987, GERRITSEN II, p. 3.
4   Equal Treatment Committee, 25 August 1988, GERRITSEN II, p. 26.
5   See e.g. Equal Treatment Committee, 25 August 1988, GERRITSEN II, p. 26.
6   HR, 25 November 1988, NJ 1989, 730 (*Riete Pot*).
7   Equal Treatment Committee, GERRITSEN I, p. 142.

used implicitly or explicitly and where moreover it was apparent from other data that those who were affected were mainly women.[1]

3.9.3   NIGHT-WORK

There is no relevant law in the Netherlands on this point.

3.9.4   PART-TIME WORK

Article 9(3) of the Equal Treatment Act provides that the pay of a part-time worker should be calculated in proportionate terms to the wages of a full-time worker.

3.9.5   RED CIRCLES

The Equal Treatment Committee has held that pay differences due to the fact that the man with whom the woman compared herself was partially disabled and received higher wages to supplement his income to the level of his former pay were legitimate.[2]

3.9.6   OTHER REASONS

Other reasons which may justify pay differentials between men and women are: (a) pay differentials based on a temporary provision; (b) work experience;[3] and (c) age.[4]

---

1   Equal Treatment Committee, Annual Report, 1988-1989, p. 96.
2   Equal Treatment Committee, 19 March 1982, GERRITSEN I, p. 146.
3   HR, 25 November 1988, NJ 1989, 730 (*Riete Pot*); see GERRITSEN II, p. 80.
4   *Oordelenbundel*, 1991, p. 240.

4. EQUAL TREATMENT

4.1 PRINCIPLE

The principle of art. 1637ij of the Civil Code and art. 1a of the Equal Treatment Act is that no direct or indirect distinction may be made between men and women in relation to employment, or access to employment.

4.2 EXCEPTIONS

The exceptions to the equal treatment principle are contained in art. 1637ij of the Civil Code and arts 1a(3), 3(2) and 5(1)-(3) of the Equal Treatment Act. These exceptions are:

(a) where sex is a determining factor;
(b) when, in the case of recruitment, exceptions are permitted under the Equal Treatment Act or other legislation;
(c) in circumstances involving the protection of women, especially in relation to pregnancy and maternity;
(d) where the aim is to place female employees in a privileged position in order to remove *de facto* inequalities.

The Equal Treatment Act allows exceptions to the equal treatment principle only if the distinction made has the object of placing women in a privileged position in order to remove *de facto* inequalities and in jobs and training for jobs where sex is a determining factor.

4.2.1 EXCLUSIONS

See §4.2 above, and §4.2.2 below.

4.2.2 SEX AS A DETERMINING FACTOR

The Equal Treatment Act, as amended, allows exceptions from the equal treatment rule where sex is a determining factor in the following cases:

(a) in religious offices;
(b) in the occupational activities of actors, actresses, singers, dancers or performers, in so far as these activities are related to the interpretation of certain parts;
(c) in other occupational activities designated by a Regulation (see art. 5(3)).

The Equal Treatment legislation originally did not include a list of occupations for which sex is a determining factor. The Act only stated that the principle was not applicable in cases where a person's sex is a determining factor. The Equal Treatment Committee therefore only permitted exceptions in exceptional cases. Preference for men in this context has only been allowed in a case where the employer wanted the employees to perform night work, which at the time was still forbidden for women.[1] In a number of cases the Committee has held that the fact that a number of women were not able to perform heavy work was not a sufficient reason to exclude women. Women who have the necessary strength and are willing to perform the job are not to be excluded.[2]

Since the amendment of the Equal Treatment Act on 1 July 1989 this exception is embodied in art. 5(3). A list based on art. 5(3) of the Equal Treatment Act (a list which is equally applicable to art. 1637ij of the Civil Code) has been put into force in a Regulation.[3]

4.2.2.1 Lists

The list referred to above, contained in the Regulation on occupations for which sex may constitute a determining factor, contains the exhaustive enumeration of the occupational activities and training which may be considered as those for which sex is a determining factor. The categories mentioned in the list are:

(a) occupations which for physical reasons can only be exercised by persons of a particular sex;
(b) occupations of male or female models who show certain garments by wearing them;
(c) occupations of models for artists, photographers, film-makers, hairdressers, make-up experts and beauty specialists;
(d) occupations within private households which involve personal service, care, nursing or bringing up of or help for one or more persons;
(e) occupations which involve personal care, nursing or help to persons, if the proper performance of the job within the whole of the organization makes it necessary that it is performed by a person of a particular sex;
(f) occupations which involve the attendance or treatment of persons, if because of a serious risk of embarrassment to these persons the proper performance of the job within the whole of the organization makes it necessary that it is performed by a person of a particular sex;
(g) occupations the practice or performance of which is prohibited by law for persons of a particular sex so as to further the protection at work of persons of that sex;

---

1   Equal Treatment Committee, 29 March 1985, GERRITSEN I, p. 375.
2   GERRITSEN I, p. 35-36.
3   Stb 1989, 207.

(h) occupations which are practised;
- in other Member States of the European Communities, if in the Member State concerned the occupations are reserved for persons of a particular sex, pursuant to the Directive of the Council of the European Communities of 9 February 1976 (76/207/EEC);
- in countries which are not Member States of the European Communities, if the applicable law reserves these occupations for persons of a particular sex;
(i) occupations in the Armed Forces, to be designated by the Minister for Defence.

There are no decisions of the courts as yet on this point.

4.2.2.2 Genuine occupational qualification

See §4.2.2.1 above.

4.2.2.3 Authenticity

The exceptions mentioned under art. 5(3) of the Equal Treatment Act were already included in the Equal Treatment Act as it read before 1 July 1989. They are considered to be obvious cases where sex is a determining factor. The enumeration has, as of 1 July 1989, been made more complete, and corresponds with that provided in the Belgian Royal Decree of 8 February 1979. The similarity, however, is not complete. In the Belgian provision the relevant clause excludes jobs where the task is 'to interpret a male or female part'. In the Netherlands it is considered that it is an aspect of artistic freedom, included in art. 7 of the Constitution, to be free to permit a male or female part to be interpreted by a person of the other sex.[1] The exceptions, mentioned in the list of occupations for which a person's sex is a determining factor, are not absolute and are determined by the criterion of authenticity.[2]

4.2.2.4 Security

Security is not relevant to the identification of occupational activities for which a person's sex may be considered a determining factor. The activities indicated under head (i) of §4.2.2.1 above are not designated for reasons of safety, but are only based on physical or practical reasons.[3] Moreover, the Minister for Defence is supposed to use his powers of designation very restrictively.

---

1 TK 19 908, 3, p. 22.
2 TK 19 908, 6, p. 31.
3 TK 19 908, 6, p. 6.

4.2.2.5   Religion

An exception to the equal treatment rule for religious offices is not provided for in the list given above, but mentioned in the Equal Treatment Act itself. The exception is derived from the principle of freedom of religion and philosophy of life.[1] In one case[2] where a Roman Catholic woman wanted to be admitted to training as a deacon, an office not open to women in the Roman Catholic church, the Equal Treatment Committee considered churches to be free to open spiritual offices to persons of one sex only. The Committee had no power to judge the correctness of an interpretation of the creed of any church.

4.2.2.6   Decency and privacy

Physical education teachers

Physical education teachers do not appear in the list under the occupations for which a person's sex is a determining factor.

Hospitals and midwives

The occupations mentioned under subparagraphs (d), (e) and (f) at §4.2.2.1 above may be relevant for employment in hospitals or the occupation of midwife, although these are not explicitly mentioned, and the matters of decency and privacy may also be applicable. The latter exception may also be allowed in other institutions. Generally, this matter relates to people who work in institutions which are charged with care, nursing or education, or assistance, and where the work within the organization makes it necessary that the job is done by someone of a particular sex. This may be particularly relevant where the persons receiving care or assistance are abused women, or in cases of treatment for patients with serious sexual disorders. In some therapies and in telephone help services the sex of the helper may also be an important factor. This exception also makes it possible to keep a balance within youth establishments between the number of male and female group leaders, although this would have to be for pedagogical reasons. The nature of the work has to be mentioned clearly in the text of any advertisement, and must include the reason for which an exception to the equal treatment rule is made.

Embarrassment

Embarrassment is relevant to the exception mentioned under subparagraph (f) in the list at §4.2.2.1 above. It concerns work where persons are treated or attended for whom serious feelings of embarrassment play a role. It has to be work which, from the perspective of the organization as a

---

1   TK 19 908, 3, p. 21.
2   2 July, 1992: see Equal Treatment Committee, Ordeel 399-92-38, Annual Report, 1992, p. 158.

whole, has to be performed by a person of a particular sex, as for instance in the case of a security officer who has the task of carrying out body searches.

Privacy

Privacy plays a role in the exception mentioned under subparagraph (d) in the list at §4.2.2.1 above. The exception relates to work in private households which consists of serving, caring for, attending to the education of, or giving help to one or more persons. This relates to work in the intimate sphere, where, amongst other factors, physical contact may play a role. Examples are private nurses, female companions or baby-sitters.

Cooks, cleaners, chauffeurs or gardeners do not fall under this exception. The nature of the work and the conditions under which it is done (i.e. in private households) have to be mentioned in any advertisements published.[1]

4.2.2.7   Single-sex establishments

No explicit exception is made for single-sex establishments.

4.3   TERRITORIAL SCOPE

Work outside the Netherlands may be excepted from the equal treatment rule, even if Dutch law is applicable. The exception is only allowed if the law of the country where the work is performed reserves the work for persons of a particular sex.

4.4   PERSONAL SCOPE

4.4.1   EMPLOYEES

The application of the Act on Contracts of Employment (*Wet op de Arbeidsovereenkomst*), of which art. 1637ij of the Civil Code is a part, is limited to employees with a contract of employment, that is to say an agreement under which one party (the employee) undertakes to perform work in the service of the other party (the employer) at specified times in return for remuneration (art. 1637a of the Civil Code). Article 1b of the Equal Treatment Act provides that if an individual, body corporate or a competent authority allows a person to perform work in their service in any way other than under a contract of employment or appointment as a civil servant, art. 1637ij of the Civil Code similarly applies. Article 1b thus broadens the scope of the equal treatment legislation to include those working in such service. A significant group of workers however remains outside the scope of the equal treatment legislation because of the fact that they are considered *not* to perform their tasks in the service of an employer.

---

[1]   *Handleiding voor het opstellen van personeelsadvertenties,* Ministerie van Sociale Zaken en Wergelegenheid, 's-Gravenhage, August 1989.

Article 1b of the Equal Treatment Act could therefore be said to bring only a small group (for instance persons who are employed while receiving a social security benefit) within the scope of the Act. Since home-based workers and casual workers are mostly female, the application of the equal treatment legislation would be especially important. This group, however, remains outside the scope of the Act.

It should be pointed out that possibly a number of persons, excluded from the scope of the national legislation, can nevertheless claim equal pay under art. 119 of the EEC Treaty.

4.4.2   INDEPENDENT CONTRACTORS

Article 2 of the Equal Treatment Act has the same effect for independent contractors (in particular members of the liberal professions) as art. 1637ij(1) of the Civil Code has for employees.

4.4.3   HOME WORKERS

Some home workers are employed on a contract of employment as described in art. 1637a of the Civil Code; in those cases art. 1637ij(1) applies. In other cases the position of the home worker does not fall within the description of art. 1637a of the Civil Code. The requirement of being 'in service' in particular seems to be absent in a number of cases, since home workers are usually free to choose their working hours and their workplace, and do not receive instructions as to how the work has to be performed. Such home workers are not within the scope of art. 1637ij of the Civil Code and are equally excluded from the scope of the Equal Treatment Act.

4.4.4   PUBLIC SECTOR

Workers in the public sector are covered by the Equal Treatment Act, notably by art. 1a. This provision also covers military personnel.

4.4.5   DOMESTIC EMPLOYEES

Domestic employees are not excluded from the scope of art. 1637ij of the Civil Code, since they are usually employed under a contract of employment.

4.4.6   NON-EMPLOYED POPULATION

Only people who work for remuneration are entitled to equal treatment. Therefore, the non-employed population is not covered by this legislation.

4.5   ACTIVITIES COVERED

The activities performed under a contract of employment, or under an appointment as a civil servant or military officer or an employment relationship where a person is in the service of somebody else, are covered by art. 1637ij of the Civil Code and by the Equal Treatment Act.

Article 3 of the Equal Treatment Act, which contains the equal treatment rule for recruitment procedures, refers to 'employment'. This term has a broader meaning than contract of employment and appointment as a civil servant. Methods of employment involving participation in the labour process in a similar way should be considered as employment within the meaning of art. 3.[1]

Article 2 of the Equal Treatment Act covers the liberal professions. The provision prohibits discrimination between men and women in relation to access to and the possibilities of practice and development within the professions.

Article 4 of the Equal Treatment Act provides that vocational guidance and training are also covered by the equal treatment principle.

4.6   COMPARATOR

It is not clear (as it was in the equal pay legislation of 1975) with whom a person has to compare herself or himself in order to establish an equal treatment entitlement. The parliamentary documents of the Equal Treatment Act as it read in 1980 make clear that, since art. 1637ij of the Civil Code is directed at the employer, a comparison is only possible with a person who is employed by the same employer as the complainant.[2] However, it is questionable whether it is necessary to make a comparison with a person of the other sex: where, for instance, a woman is refused a job because of her pregnancy, is it necessary for her claim to be successful that a man got the job, or is it sufficient that she was turned down because of a discriminatory motive? This question, initially raised in 1983, was put to the ECJ by the *Hoge Raad* in the *Dekker* case,[3] and was answered by the Court in the negative.[4]

4.7   HIRING

In Dutch equal treatment legislation a distinction has been drawn between hiring, which is regulated in art. 1637ij(1) of the Civil Code for

---

[1]   TK 19 908, 3, p. 14.
[2]   TK 15 400, 6, p. 15.
[3]   HR, 24 June 1988, NJ 1988, 1002.
[4]   [1990] ECR I-3941, NJ 1992, 224 (ECJ).

employees and in art. 1a(1) of the Equal Treatment Act for Civil Servants, and recruitment, which is regulated by art. 3 of the Equal Treatment Act for both categories. There is some uncertainty as to when art. 1637ij of the Civil Code and art. 1a of the Equal Treatment Act are applicable, and when art. 3 of the Equal Treatment Act applies. This is crucial for determining the sanctions which may result from violations of the rule. From the parliamentary history[1] of the legislation it is clear that the legislature intended to include in art. 3 of the Equal Treatment Act all activities in relation to hiring, including both recruitment and selection procedures. No distinction was made between the internal and the external stages of the selection procedure, nor between the procedure and the actual choice of a person. Now that the whole procedure is covered by art. 3 of the Equal Treatment Act, should it be supposed, as van der Weele[2] does, that art. 1637ij of the Civil Code (and art. 1a of the Equal Treatment Act) only bears upon questions such as hiring for a definite or an indefinite period of time, with or without a trial period? There appear to be two grounds for suggesting that art. 1637ij of the Civil Code and art. 1a of the Equal Treatment Act also refer to the actual decision to select or not to select a certain candidate.

Firstly, the texts are clear: art. 1637ij(1) of the Civil Code and art. 1a(1) of the Equal Treatment Act speak of 'entering into a contract of employment' and 'appointment to a post of civil servant', not of 'entering into a contract of employment under certain conditions' and 'appointment under certain conditions'. In the second place, from the parliamentary papers it is clear that both art. 3 and art. 1637ij(1) were meant to be applications of (inter alia) art. 3 of Directive 76/207/EEC.[3] The Equal Treatment Committee is not very consistent in its choice of art. 3 of the Equal Treatment Act or art. 1637ij(1) of the Civil Code when the evaluation of such situations is under discussion. The courts appear to be inclined to apply art. 1637ij of the Civil Code.

It could be said that both the wording of art. 1637ij(1) and the situation in practice make it possible to distinguish between recruitment and selection on the one hand and the eventual decision to employ on the other. If both art. 3 of the Equal Treatment Act and art. 1637ij refer to hiring, it seems that art. 1637ij of the Civil Code (and art. 1a of the Equal Treatment Act) refers more to the situation where the employer makes a decision relating to one, individual, person.[4]

In the amended Equal Treatment Act a distinction is made between recruitment and selection. Recruitment is covered by the words 'procedure for the purpose of filling a vacancy'.

---

1   TK 15 400, 3, p. 16.
2   J.J. VAN DER WEELE, *Wet Gelijke Behandeling van Mannen en Vrouwen*, Deventer, 1983, p. 88.
3   TK 15 400, 3, p. 10.
4   See I.P. ASSCHER-VONK, 'Toegang tot de dienstbetrekking via gelijke behandeling', in *Schetsen voor Bakels*, Kluwer, 1987, p. 1.

4.7.1 RECRUITMENT METHODS

The choice of the words 'procedure for the purpose of filling a vacancy', which replaced the former 'advertisement' in art. 3 of the Equal Treatment Act, should make clear that the text of the Act as it now reads refers not only to the job offer in an advertisement, but also to other ways of overtly offering a job. Internal recruitment in particular is therefore covered.[1]

4.7.2 ADVERTISEMENTS

Article 3(2) of the Equal Treatment Act provides that there may only be a reference to the exceptions allowed by the law if in the public offer of the job the reason for the distinction has been explicitly explained. Article 3(3) provides (and this applies especially to advertisements) that the offer of the job must be made (in relation both to the text and the design) in such a way that it is clear that both men and women will be considered. The term 'design' is rather broad and refers *inter alia* to lay-out and illustrations. This does not mean that only illustrations in which persons of both sexes are shown are allowed, nor that in cases where illustrations show persons of both sexes the job offer is *per se* in accordance with the law. The job offer as a whole must make it clear that not only persons of one sex will be considered. Illustrations will have to be considered in relation to the rest of the offer. This also applies to the use of male or female pronouns.[2]

In 1988 the Equal Treatment Committee wrote 219 times, and in the first half of 1989 it wrote 99 times, to advertisers who were in breach of the Equal Treatment Act to draw their attention to the Act. These advertisements had been sent to the Committee by third parties. A note is made of all advertisers written to, so that the Committee can check whether the infringement is repeated.[3] In the Annual Report 1992, only 37 cases concerned advertisements in breach of the provisions of the Equal Treatment Act.

4.7.3 JOB TITLE

Article 3(4) of the Equal Treatment Act refers to job titles for which both male and female versions exist, and for which there are neutral job titles. No special form is prescribed, but it provides that either the male and the female forms should be used together, or that in other cases it should be explicitly mentioned that both men and women will be considered.[4]

---

[1] TK 19 908, 3, p. 16.
[2] TK 19 908, 3, p. 17.
[3] Equal Treatment Committee, Annual Report, 1988-1989, p. 50.
[4] TK 19 908, 3, p. 17.

4.7.4   JOB DESCRIPTION

The information leaflet issued by the Government about equal treatment in hiring[1] refers to the issue of job descriptions. The leaflet states that only requirements which are relevant to the job may be mentioned in advertisements. In stating these requirements, there must not be any distinction made between men and women, unless it concerns, in the case of indirect distinctions, genuine job qualifications. No requirements may be set out in advertisements which for obvious reasons may discourage men or women as a group from applying.

4.7.5   SELECTION ARRANGEMENTS

Selection arrangements have been discussed in the report of a special committee.[2] The yardstick used was the 'right to a fair chance of appointment'. This means that all potential candidates must be able to learn of the vacancy, and that those candidates who are more or less equally qualified or eligible should have an equal chance of being appointed. The report stated that job descriptions and requirements should be clearly formulated, and that all requirements should be genuine and relevant. A number of factors may, generally speaking, be considered as not relevant, and no demands relating to them may be made unless it is clear that they are necessary. These factors are age, sex, marital status, sexual orientation, personal features, psychiatric history, medical history, nationality, race or colour, social or regional background, criminal record, religious, political or philosophical persuasion, membership of a trade union or other organization, and unemployment.

The *Stichting van de Arbeid* (Foundation of Labour), in which the central organizations of trade unions and employers are represented, made a recommendation in 1991, following other recommendations in this field, to 'keep in mind the objective requirements of a job, offer equivalent workers equal opportunities for work and equal opportunities within the labour organization, not to consider factors such as age, sex, sexual orientation, marital status, religious or philosophical persuasion, colour, race or ethnic origin, nationality or political choices'. In a number of collective agreements this recommendation, or elements of it, have been followed.[3] It should be pointed out that these provisions in collective agreements have been formulated other than in a binding way: it is not clear whether an individual person could use such a provision as a basis for a claim for equal treatment.

---

1   Ministerie van Sociale Zaken en Werkgelegenheid, August 1989.
2   *Eindrapport Commissie Selectieprocedure: Een sollicitant is ook een mens*, 's-Gravenhage, 1977.
3   I.P. ASSCHER-VONK, *Toegang tot de dienstbetrekking*, Alphen aan den Rijn, 1989, p. 33.

In 1982 the *Stichting van de Arbeid* made a recommendation about selection arrangements.[1] Two principles are worth noting in that recommendation, these being the criterion of suitability, and that the rights of the applicant must be observed. These rights are: a reasonable chance of being appointed; the right to information; the right of privacy; the right to confidential treatment of personal data; the right to efficient selection arrangements; and the right of complaint.

In a number of collective agreements elements of the recommendation have been followed. A study by the DCA[2] shows that to be the case in 11 of the 82 collective agreements examined (applicable to 25 per cent of the employees).

4.7.6   TERMS ON WHICH A JOB IS OFFERED

As set out above, the terms on which a job is offered are covered by art. 1637ij of the Civil Code. The Equal Treatment Committee advised on this point on 23 April 1985.[3] In that case a woman was offered a job; when, at the medical examination before the contract of employment was entered into, it appeared that she was pregnant, the job was offered for a period of seven months. The Equal Treatment Committee deemed this to have been contrary to art. 1637ij(1) of the Civil Code.

4.7.7   REFUSAL OR DELIBERATE OMISSION TO OFFER A JOB

The question of a deliberate omission or refusal to offer a job was illustrated in a case where a couple applied for a franchising contract. The employer concluded a written contract of employment with the man. The woman had to counter-sign the contract of employment. The Equal Treatment Committee ruled that the fact that in the contract of employment the term 'wife of the employee' was used amounted to discrimination between married and unmarried persons. The choice of the man as the party to the contract of employment was a form of unequal treatment. The wife had, because of her sex, no realistic chance of being a party to the contract. The Equal Treatment Committee declared this to be unequal treatment between men and women.[4]

---

1   *Stichting van de Arbeid*, 21 July 1982.
2   DCA, *Werving en selectie in CAO's (eindrapportage)*, Ministerie van Sociale Zaken en Werkgelegenheid, 's-Gravenhage, 1988.
3   GERRITSEN I, p. 165.
4   Equal Treatment Committee, 8 August 1988, GERRITSEN II, p. 35.

4.8   WORKING CONDITIONS

4.8.1   RELATION TO PAY

A number of cases brought before the Equal Treatment Committee have been concerned with working conditions which were related to pay. In one case, decided on 13 February 1981, there was a difference in the treatment of part-time and full-time employees concerning the payment of sickness compensation by the employer. The Equal Treatment Committee did not consider this to amount to indirect discrimination because there were both male and female part-time employees and both male and female full-time employees in the employer's service.[1]

In a case decided in 1983[2] female employees were paid, in addition to their monthly pay, a seven per cent holiday allowance, whereas the male employees got 14 times the monthly pay *per annum* plus a bonus. This, it was decided, was direct discrimination and a breach of the equal treatment legislation.

Another case, in the last instance decided by the *Hoge Raad* on 25 November 1988, should also be mentioned. The employee's last pay was used as a criterion for the level of pay at which the employee was to commence employment. The *Hoge Raad* held that if other working experience was left out of consideration in choosing the level of pay, there was no objective justification for the indirect discrimination caused by the use of the criterion of the last pay. The fact that this criterion may be used to avoid the situation where a person entering employment earns less pay, compared with that earned in a former job, is not an objective justification.

In another case the allowance for weekend service was subject to a maximum sum in the collective agreement for swimming pool staff. Weekend service was almost exclusively performed by part-time staff. The Equal Treatment Committee[3] stated that because of the fact that it was generally known that part-timers were mostly women, there was a suspicion of indirect discrimination. The Committee stated that only reasons which were relevant to the functioning of the organization could be accepted as objective justification. The removal of differences in pay did not amount to justification, nor did the improvement of the position of part-time staff in other respects justify the discrimination.

Pursuant to the collective agreement for child-care, breadwinners received a higher allowance for the costs of health insurance than that received by non-breadwinners. The employer argued in favour of this scheme

---

1   GERRITSEN I, p. 173.
2   GERRITSEN I, p. 177.
3   Equal Treatment Committee, 7 July 1986, GERRITSEN I, p. 218.

by stating that private health insurance, as distinct from the State health insurance, did not recognize a premium-free insurance family. According to the Equal Treatment Committee,[1] the preference for breadwinners in the agreement amounted to a suspicion of indirect discrimination; the intention of the employer to compensate for the costs incurred did not justify this.

4.8.2 EDUCATION AND TRAINING

There is no relevant law in the Netherlands on this point

4.8.3 ACCESS TO BENEFITS, FACILITIES, SERVICES, PROMOTION

Two cases in which the Equal Treatment Committee had to give its opinion concerning promotion are relevant under this heading. The first was decided on 13 May 1982, and concerned a department of six employees. The three men were promoted, whereas the three women were not. The department head had made the decision without using an objective system. Nevertheless, the Committee did not hold that the employer had committed direct or indirect discrimination.[2]

In the other case, decided on 7 February 1986, a woman applied (internally) for a job as material handler. Her application was turned down at the pre-selection stage because the employer expected problems in relation to her ability to exercise natural leadership and social communication. Also, the employer expected that the woman would not have time for further study, although this was denied by the woman. The Committee noted that the woman had not worked in a leadership role. It also became clear that from 1983 she had been criticized concerning her co-operation with and influence on colleagues, which criticism had been made known to the woman. The man who was appointed was already experienced in material handling and leadership and worked in harmony with his colleagues. The Committee held that the employer had not discriminated between men and women in turning down the woman.[3]

4.9 EXCLUSION, DISMISSAL OR OTHER DETRIMENT

Selection for dismissal based on seniority

The Equal Treatment Committee has held that a departure from the practice of selection by seniority, where it is to the detriment of women, indicates a suspicion of indirect discrimination.[4]

---

[1] Equal Treatment Committee, 22 October 1986, GERRITSEN I, p. 226.
[2] GERRITSEN I, p. 228.
[3] GERRITSEN II, p. 230.
[4] Equal Treatment Committee, 23 January 1985, GERRITSEN I, p. 277.

On the other hand, the application of a seniority rule may also give rise to a suspicion of indirect discrimination, although one for which the absence of alternatives may be a justification.[1] The Committee has also ruled that the practice of giving credit for the time spent on compulsory military service when applying the seniority rule is direct discrimination.[2]

In one case where selection for dismissal was decided by counting years of service, whereby any year in which employees had worked less than half time was counted as a half year, the Equal Treatment Committee ruled that this practice was indirect discrimination, not justified by the argument put forward by the employer that part-time staff, by way of compensation, had enjoyed more favourable conditions of work. The Committee argued that the aim of giving more women a chance to be hired did not justify the practice of letting them be the first to be dismissed.[3]

Dismissal because of pregnancy

In general terms, under Dutch dismissal law a dismissal during pregnancy is null and void (art. 1639h of the Civil Code). Dismissal during a trial period or probation, which may be of a maximum duration of two months, is always possible, even in cases where dismissal is otherwise forbidden (for example, during pregnancy). There has been an extensive debate, prompted by an opinion of the Equal Treatment Committee of 7 September 1982, as to whether art. 1637ij of the Civil Code (which, *inter alia*, provides for equal treatment in dismissal) means that during the trial period dismissal during pregnancy may be allowed, but dismissal *because of pregnancy* is not. The *Kantonrechter* of Nijmegen held that the employer may not use the trial period to terminate an employment relationship because of a pregnancy, because such a course of action amounts to unlawful discrimination between women and men.[4] On appeal this judgment was confirmed.[5]

Dismissal procedures

In general terms, under Dutch dismissal law an employer needs the permission of a Government official to be able to terminate an employment relationship.[6] In practice, this rule has provided protection for employees against unfair dismissal. Excluded from the scope of the BBA are, *inter alia*, part-time workers who are employed in a private household. This exclusion,

---

1   Equal Treatment Committee, 7 February 1986, GERRITSEN I, p. 296.
2   *Ibid.*
3   Equal Treatment Committee, 7 July 1986, GERRITSEN I, p. 300.
4   *Kantonrechter*, Nijmegen, 25 July 1986, Prg 1987, p. 2622.
5   *Rechtbank*, Arnhem, 24 December 1987, NJ 1988, 309.
6   See BBA, art. 6.

which mainly affects women, is also to be found in some social security Acts (see §5.4 below). It could be argued that this exclusion is indirectly discriminatory,[1] since the arguments (administrative trouble for the employer, for example) might not be thought to be very convincing or to meet the standards which the ECJ has set for objective justification.

4.10   INSTRUCTIONS TO DISCRIMINATE

There is no relevant law on this point in the Netherlands.

4.11   PRESSURE TO DISCRIMINATE

There is no relevant law on this point in the Netherlands.

4.12   DISCRIMINATION BY AN EMPLOYEE
OR A TRADE UNION

There is no relevant law on this point in the Netherlands.

4.13   DISCRIMINATORY PRACTICES

There is no relevant law (other than that which has already been discussed under other headings) on this point in the Netherlands.

4.14   SPECIAL TREATMENT

4.14.1   PROTECTIVE LEGISLATION

4.14.1.1 Pregnancy and maternity

Provision for the protection of women in relation to pregnancy and maternity is contained in protective legislation and in the regulation of the contract of employment, as well as in collective agreements. The protection of women in relation to pregnancy and maternity in social security is discussed at §5.4.3 below.

The relevant protective legislation is to be found in art. 11(1) of the *Arbeidswet* (Labour Act), which prohibits a woman from working for a period of eight weeks after her confinement. It is possible to deduct from the eight-week period a maximum of two weeks during which the woman did not work before her confinement. The prohibition of dismissal during pregnancy and the provisions of art. 1639h of the Civil Code relating to dismissal because of confinement should also be noted.

---

[1]   See I.P. ASSCHER-VONK, 'Wijziging van het BBA', NJB 1987, p 235.

The rules which exist to protect women during pregnancy and maternity allow for exceptions to the equal treatment principle. Rules of this nature are not often found in collective agreements.[1] An example of a condition of this nature in an individual contract was found in one case, decided by the Equal Treatment Committee on 3 April 1989.[2] An employer had included a provision in the conditions of employment for parental leave for women, up to a maximum of one year and directly following the maternity leave. A male employee asked the employer for parental leave in order to be able to care for his new-born child. The employer refused. The Equal Treatment Committee argued that the employer had discriminated between men and women. However, the Committee held that this practice was permitted as women were under-represented in the employer's service and because one of the problems for women was the combination of professional activities and childcare.

The right to breast-feed a baby is laid down in art. 11(2) of the *Arbeidswet*. This provision states that the employer must facilitate a female employee who has a breast-fed child by giving proper accommodation to nurse the baby. This means that, according to case law, the employer has to make sure there is a suitable room to nurse the baby, and to let the mother nurse the child during working hours.[3] The employer does not have to provide a room where the baby can stay between feedings: it is the mother's responsibility to arrange that the child is present at the time of the feedings. Only when there is no accommodation in the plant does the employer have to give the woman the opportunity to nurse her baby at home.

4.14.1.2 Parental leave and similar measures

See §4.14.1.1 above.

4.14.1.3 Difficult or unpleasant working conditions

See §4.14.1.4 below.

4.14.1.4 Health and safety

In the protective legislation no special provision is made for difficult or unpleasant working conditions or health and safety. Article 25 of the *Arbeidswet* provides only for the regulation of overtime. Overtime worked by women is subject to more restrictions than overtime worked by men.

The fact that work is heavy, unpleasant or unsafe is repeatedly used by employers to justify their preference for men. This cannot, however, be used

---

1   DCA-Rapport, *Emancipatie in arbeidsorganisaties*, 1992.
2   GERRITSEN II, p. 63.
3   Hof Amsterdam, 30 May 1980, NJ 1981, 136.

as a reason for discrimination in recruitment, and any attempt by an employer to do so will be rejected by the Equal Treatment Committee.

4.14.2 POSITIVE ACTION

4.14.2.1 Definition

A number of definitions of positive action are used. In the *Nota positieve actie-programma's voor vrouwen in arbeidsorganisaties*,[1] on which the *Sociaal-economische Raad* (Social and Economic Council) advised on 16 February 1990, it was stated that a positive action plan consisted of coherent and integrated measures aimed at improving the position of women in an organization, with the management taking responsibility for the introduction of the measures within the time limits set and for the periodical evaluation of the measures, assessed in the light of concrete and, where possible, quantified objectives included in the plan.

In the framework of the equal treatment legislation in the Netherlands the term 'preferential treatment' is more common. Preferential treatment, as an exception to the equal treatment principle, may be part of a positive action programme in the broader sense. Preferential treatment is unequal treatment which aims to put women in a privileged position in order to overcome existing inequalities.

In the Explanatory Memorandum to the 1989 Amendment of the Equal Treatment Act the Government set out a number of criteria which are relevant to the admissibility of preferential treatment. The Equal Treatment Committee is guided by the Explanatory Memorandum in testing the admissibility of preferential treatment. The criteria applied are:

–   the arrears of women should be shown, by kind and level of job;
–   the most effective intensity of preferential treatment should be chosen, having regard to the kind and level of job;
–   if preferential treatment in recruitment is applied, the policy should be made known in an advertisement.[2]

There is a point to be noted on the burden of proof. The onus seems to be upon the employer to disprove that women are in arrears.

---

1   Letter of the Minister for Social Affairs and Employment to the *Sociaal-economische Raad* and the *Emancipatieraad* of 30 November 1987.
2   I.P. ASSCHER-VONK and K. WENTHOLT, *Wet gelijke behandeling van mannen en vrouwen*, Deventer, 1994, p. 61.

4.14.2.2 Areas

Positive action plans in enterprises are encouraged by the Government.[1] However, the Government does not take the view that it should force organizations to use positive action plans. Positive action plans should be conceived within an organization. For a positive action plan to be successful it is important that there is broad support for it within the organization. Moreover, in the Netherlands there is little practical experience of positive action plans. The Government proposes to follow a supportive policy, consisting of research, information and grants. Conditions attached to subsidies are thought of as a possibility; contract compliance is, for the time being, thought too extreme a measure.

4.14.2.3 Means

It is clear from an Equal Treatment Committee opinion that training may be used as a way of correcting existing inequalities.[2]

4.14.2.4 Constitutional or legal problems

At the annual meeting of the *Nederlandse Juristen-Vereniging* (Dutch lawyers' association) of 1989, positive discrimination was a subject for discussion. The legal and constitutional problems of positive discrimination were discussed broadly. The discussions were centred on the more general problems: the admissibility of the exception as laid down in the Equal Treatment Act in its current form appears to be generally accepted.

---

1   See §4.14.2.1 above.
2   Opinion No 87-8 of 16 June 1978.

5.   SOCIAL SECURITY

5.1   DEFINITION OF SOCIAL SECURITY

There is no unanimous view in Dutch legal literature as to the way social security should be defined. One definition worth quoting is that by Levenbach, who states that social security consists of 'the entirety of institutions and regulations which provide a group ... with welfare facilities in the event of circumstances concerning them personally, which may concern persons belonging to that group and which make those facilities desirable'.[1] Jaspers and Riphagen state that 'social security aims at the provision of an income guarantee to those who are not or no longer able to provide themselves with subsistence by working'.[2] The latter definition seems to leave no room for health insurance and family benefits, both undoubtedly part of the Dutch system of social security. Noordam adds, to a definition which is essentially similar to that of Jaspers and Riphagen, that social security also has to set off income deficiencies. Available income may be insufficient for specific costs, for instance medical costs, housing or child support. In such cases social security supplements income or pays the costs concerned.[3]

5.1.1   STATUTORY SOCIAL SECURITY

Although it is not apparent from these definitions, attention has always been focused almost exclusively on statutory social security. A number of Acts cover the different fields in which social security is needed, such as old age, widowhood, sickness, accident, invalidity, unemployment, health costs, and children's allowance. Nowadays the cost of further studies or training is also reckoned to be part of the risks for which statutory social security may compensate.

5.1.2   OCCUPATIONAL SOCIAL SECURITY

Occupational social security has, as part of the conditions of work, always been embodied in collective agreements. Even if the benefits were financed in the same way as the benefits in statutory social security schemes (as was the case for instance with extra sickness benefits over and above the statutory 70 per cent of normal wages) the basic decision was made in collective bargaining. Old-age pensions were similarly negotiated through collective bargaining between employers' and employees' representatives.

---

[1]   M.G. LEVENBACH, *Nederlands Bestuursrecht*, Alphen aan den Rijn, 1964.

[2]   A.P.C.M. JASPERS and J. RIPHAGEN, *Schets van het sociaal zekerheidsrecht*, (2nd ed.), Deventer, 1989.

[3]   F.M. NOORDAM, *Inleiding Sociale-Zekerheidsrecht*, Deventer, 1994, p. 21.

5.1.3 SOCIAL ASSISTANCE

Formerly narrow definitions of social security, which stressed that social security should be contributory, left social assistance out of their scope. Nowadays, however, social assistance is generally accepted as a part of social security.

5.1.4 PERSONS COVERED

5.1.4.1 Working population

As far as the personal scope of social security legislation is concerned, the whole of statutory social security may be divided into three parts. The first part consists of social security which covers employees and related groups: these are unemployment benefits, sickness and accident benefits, and health insurance. The second part consists of social security which is necessary for everybody and covers every resident (employees included): this includes old-age and widows' pensions, children's allowances, study costs, and invalidity benefits. The third part, social assistance, covers all Dutch persons: in other words, it uses nationality to define its scope. Members of the working population who fall within the scope of EC law are to be found in all of the groups.

The question whether Directive 79/7/EEC applies to persons who have not been part of the working population and are not seeking employment has been put to the ECJ, which issued its judgment on 27 June 1989 following questions from Dutch social security tribunals.[1] The Court ruled that the Directive does not apply to such persons.

5.1.4.2 Public or private sector

Traditionally, civil servants have had their own regulations, forming part of the conditions of their employment. The regulations provided for income in case of sickness, invalidity and unemployment. Civil servants had always been excluded from social security schemes for employees, but with the new Unemployment Act (*Werkloosheidswet*) of 1 January 1987 that exclusion was prospectively terminated, from a date to be announced by decree. It was thought that the different treatment of civil servants and employees in social security matters should gradually be abolished. The decree, however, has not yet been issued, and negotiations regarding the ending of this exclusion have been difficult.

5.1.4.3 Employees or self-employed persons

Included in the scope of the social security scheme for employees are those self-employed persons who are considered to be comparable, as far as their socio-economic position is concerned, with employees. In this way,

---

[1] *Achterberg-te Riele* v. *Sociale Verzekeringsbank, Amsterdam*, Joined Cases 48, 106 and 107/88, [1989] ECR 1963 (ECJ).

homeworkers, performing artists, travelling salesmen, etc., have been brought within the scope of the Acts.

5.1.5 BENEFITS COVERED

5.1.5.1 Contributory

Most contributory benefits (the 'classic branch' of social security) are covered by the equal treatment principle in Directive 79/7/EEC, because most contributory benefits apply to the working population. Exceptions are the survivors' benefits in the *Algemene Weduwen- en Wezenwet* (General Act on Benefits for Widows and Orphans), and the children's allowance in the *Algemene Kinderbijslagwet* (Child Benefits Act), because they cover risks outside the scope of the Directive for a group of persons who are not members of the working population. An equal treatment rule, like that contained in the International Covenant on Civil and Political Rights, does however play a role in these benefits.

5.1.5.2 Non-contributory

Non-contributory benefits are covered. They are the *Toeslagenwet* (Supplements Act), which provides supplements, depending on the family situation, added to the sickness, invalidity and unemployment benefits; and the *Wet Inkomensvoorziening Oudere en Gedeeltelijk Arbeidsongeschikte Werknemers* (IOAW: Act on Benefits for Elderly and Partially Disabled Employees), which provides benefits for older and partially disabled unemployed employees. Here the application of the equal treatment rule is difficult, because the benefits are available if the family income falls below a certain minimum. This may be considered indirectly discriminatory.

The *Wet Werkloosheidsvoorziening* (WWV: Act on Unemployment Benefits), an Act which provided for unemployment benefits (now replaced by the *Werkloosheidswet*: the Unemployment Act), is also subject to the equal treatment principle. Despite a number of legal proceedings it is still not clear how that Act can be brought into compliance with the equal treatment principle.

5.1.5.3 Means-tested

Means-tested benefits are also covered by the equal treatment rule. They are to be found in the *Algemene Bijstandswet* (ABW: Social Assistance Act), which makes provision for social assistance, and in Decrees concerning certain groups based on that Act, for instance for unemployed former employees and unemployed former self-employed persons.

5.1.5.4 Pensions

Old-age pensions are provided for in the *Algemene Ouderdomswet* (AOW: Old Age Act), which covers all residents of the Netherlands. Application of the equal treatment principle has led to an amendment of the law, effective from 1 April 1988, by which the former rule that married woman were not entitled to 50 per cent of the benefit which used to be given to the married man was abolished. If one of the spouses is younger than 65 (the statutory retirement age), a supplement of 50 per cent on the benefit of the other spouse is paid if the income of the younger spouse is below a certain level. Such provision may fall foul of the equal treatment principle, as younger spouses tend to be women rather than men. Also, more men than women have a spouse with little or no income. This means that more men than women receive a supplement to their old-age pension.

The question whether this is in breach of Directive 79/7/EEC was answered by the *Raad van Beroep* of Arnhem on 21 December 1989 in the following way. The *Raad van Beroep* stated that the question whether the supplements to the AOW were suitable and necessary to attain the objective pursued could be left open. Non-application of the provision would cause a number of practical problems for men and women. Therefore the appeal, stating that the supplements were indirectly discriminatory, was dismissed.[1]

The *Raad van Beroep* of Amsterdam submitted this question to the ECJ in 1991. The ECJ decided that there was objective justification for this rule, despite the fact that more women than men are prejudiced, and that there was therefore no indirect discrimination within the terms of the Directive.[2]

5.1.6   UNEMPLOYMENT

The *Werkloosheidswet* 1987 (WW: the Unemployment Act), satisfies the standards imposed by the equal treatment principle.

Although the *Wet Werkloosheidsvoorziening* (WWV: Act on Unemployment Benefits) has been repealed, it remains relevant to cases where the unemployment began before 1 January 1987. Originally only those married women who were considered to be breadwinners were entitled to benefits under the WWV, a requirement not applied to married men. After litigation which went as far as the ECJ changes in the law were introduced. The question remained as to the point from which a married woman was entitled to equal unemployment benefits under the WWV, and for what period. Following the judgment of the ECJ in the *Dik* case of 8 March 1988,[3]

---

1   Case AOW 88/2387, PS 1990, p. 34.
2   *Molenbroeck* v. *Bestuur van de Sociale Verzekeringsbank*, Case C-226/91, [1992] ECR I-5943; RSV 1993, 59 (ECJ).
3   *Dik* v. *College van Burgemeester en Wethouders Arnhem*, Case 80/87, [1988] ECR 1601 (ECJ).

the *Centrale Raad van Beroep*[1] held that a woman was entitled to equal rights from 23 December 1984, for the maximum time as determined by her age.

5.1.7   ACCIDENTS AT WORK

Invalidity and accidents at work are both covered by two Acts: the *Wet op de Arbeidsongeschiktheidsverzekering* (WAO: Workers' Disability Act) for employees and the *Algemene Arbeidsongeschiktheidswet* for all residents in the Netherlands. It has been questioned whether the fact that women seem to be passed as fit for work (and therefore no longer entitled to benefits) more often than men is indirect discrimination. A recent publication in this discussion was Bruinsma, Jacobi and van der Stelt.[2] Their conclusion was that the difference between men and women in invalidity benefits vanishes when one looks at men and women in comparable jobs. The differences which exist are more properly considered in this regard than attributed to discrimination. On this Hermans[3] replied that the position on the labour market or the kind of job does not seem to be the determining factor for the difference in invalidity benefits. He states that the causes of the difference are still not clear.

In relation to the *Algemene Arbeidsongeschiktheidswet* it should be noted that on 23 June 1992 the *Centrale Raad van Beroep* ruled[4] that in its current form the income threshold for eligibility for benefits under the Act was prejudicial to women and indirectly discriminatory.

5.2   SOCIAL SECURITY DIRECTIVES AND OTHER LEGISLATION

5.2.1   ARTICLE 119 OF THE EEC TREATY

Article 119 is especially important for equal treatment in occupational social security. The essential question is whether the benefits concerned may be regarded as pay. Loenen[5] states that art. 119 may be relied upon when there are differences in the employers' contributions, differences in the percentage per annum, differences in the admittance age or restrictions in admittance for women. Van Eekeren[6] states that it is important that art. 119 can be used to fight discrimination in occupational social security, while it may be a long time before Directive 86/378/EEC is implemented in national legislation and occupational social security systems are adapted to the demands of that Directive.

---

1   CRvB, 10 May 1989, *Rechtspraak Nemesis*, 1989, p. 99.
2   SMA 1989, pp 91-109.
3   SMA 1989, p. 106.
4   *NJCM-Bulletin* 1993, p. 292.
5   M.L.P. LOENEN, SMA 1986, pp 390-403.
6   P.J. VAN EEKEREN, 'Ongelijke behandeling in aanvullende pensioenregelingen: oplossingen vanuit het Europese recht', SMA 1989, pp 240-248.

5.2.2   DIRECTIVE 75/117/EEC

See Chapter 3 above.

5.2.3   DIRECTIVE 76/207/EEC

The provisions of Directive 76/207/EEC prompted the Government to introduce a number of changes in legislation, among which was the revision of the *Algemene Ouderdomswet*, which formerly excluded married women from benefits.

5.2.4   DIRECTIVE 79/7/EEC

See §1.2.2.1 above, and generally Chapter 5.

5.2.5   DIRECTIVE 86/378/EEC

Draft legislation has been prepared in order to meet the requirements of the Directive of 24 July 1986.[1] The proposal is to extend art. 1637ij of the Civil Code and the Equal Treatment Act to occupational social security.

5.2.6   INTERNATIONAL COVENANT ON CIVIL AND

POLITICAL RIGHTS

In practice, the International Covenant on Civil and Political Rights is a very important source of law in fighting discrimination in the Netherlands, especially between men and women and between married persons and cohabitants. The principle contained in art. 26 is applied in cases where, because of the nature of the regulation (for instance, widowers' pensions), the EEC Directive does not apply, or where the alleged discrimination occurred before the Directive came into force, or where it does not concern discrimination between men and women, but, for instance, between married persons and cohabitants.

5.3   PROBLEMATIC CONCEPTS

5.3.1   BREADWINNER

The breadwinner concept played a role before 1 January 1987 in the rules which guaranteed minimum benefits for families. Now the breadwinner concept has been replaced by rules which make supplementary benefits conditional on the absence of income from the partner (spouse or cohabitant). Clearly, in a society where a large number of married women are still not employed (and, where they are employed, a majority work part-time) this rule may create difficulties from the point of view of indirect discrimination.

5.3.2   SOLE BREADWINNER

There is no exception of this type in Dutch social security law

---

[1]   TK 20 890.

5.4   EXCEPTIONS

Part-time employees working in private households for less than three days a week are excluded from the scope of the employees' social security scheme.

5.4.1   RETIREMENT AGE

There is no provision for such an exception in Dutch social security law.

5.4.2   SEX AS A DETERMINING FACTOR

There is no provision for such an exception in Dutch social security law.

5.4.3   PREGNANCY AND MATERNITY

Directive 79/7/EEC on equal treatment in social security permits protective measures for women on the grounds of pregnancy and maternity. In the Netherlands effect has been given to this exception in art. 19(2) of the *Ziektewet* (Sickness Benefits Act), art. 18(5) of the *Wet op de Arbeidsongeschiktheidsverzekering* (WAO: Workers' Disability Act) and art. 5(6) of the *Algemene Arbeidsongeschiktheidswet* (AAW: General Disability Act). In these provisions pregnancy and confinement, circumstances which only can affect women, are identified with sickness as a cause for incapacity.

Furthermore, during a period of six weeks before the estimated date of confinement until 10 weeks after confinement the woman is entitled to sickness benefits, irrespective of whether she is in fact unable to work. If a woman falls ill before that period, and the illness is caused by the pregnancy, the woman is entitled to sickness benefits amounting to 100 per cent of her wages (Sickness Benefits Act, art. 29a(3)).

Moreover, during this period, and until the time the woman has recovered from the confinement and pregnancy (and related ailments if that time is more than six weeks) the woman is entitled to sickness benefits amounting to 100 per cent of her wages (compared with normal sickness pay, which is 70 per cent of wages).

5.4.4   SURVIVORS' BENEFITS

This subject is excluded from the scope of Directive 79/7/EEC because it neither concerns the risks listed in art. 4, nor does it apply to members of the working population as such. Survivors' benefits are contained in the *Algemene Weduwen- en Wezenwet*. The fact that only widows were entitled to benefits under this Act led to litigation in which art. 26 of the International Covenant on Civil and Political Rights was invoked. The *Centrale Raad van Beroep* stated that the distinction between men and women in the AWW was a violation of art. 26 of the Covenant. As a consequence, men who are widowers are also entitled to a widow's pension.[1]

5.4.5 FAMILY BENEFITS

Family benefits and children's allowances do not fall within the scope of the social security Directives.

5.5 LEVELLING UP/DOWN

Nothing definite can be said about whether levelling up or down takes place. However, by an Act of 4 May 1989 the entitlement to invalidity benefits for those who became handicapped before 1 January 1979 has been made dependent on whether there has been loss of income because of the invalidity. Formerly this requirement was only made when it concerned married women. Since this was considered a breach of art. 26 of the International Covenant on Civil and Political Rights, the amendment was thought necessary. The amendment, as now in force, may be considered as amounting to a levelling down.[2]

5.6 PART-TIME WORK

The recent judgment of the ECJ, concerning invalidity benefits for part-time workers, is important.[3] The case concerned part-time workers (mainly women) who received a *pro-rata* benefit, while other persons, regardless of whether they had a large or small income, received the 'normal' benefit (70 per cent of the minimum wages). The ECJ held that this practice amounted to indirect discrimination for which there was no objective justification. The reason given, that the benefit should not exceed the former income, was rejected because for a number of full-time workers that was already the case. The *Centrale Raad van Beroep*, however, held that the provision was not in contravention of the equality principle.[4]

---

1   CRvB, 7 December 1988, RSV, 1989, p. 67.
2   L. ANDRINGA, 'A never ending story', *Rechtspraak Nemesis*, 1989, p. 181.
3   *Ruzius-Wilbrink* v. *Bestuur van de Bedrijfsvereniging voor Overheidsdiensten*, Case C-102/88, [1989] ECR 4311 (ECJ).
4   CRvB, 6 June 1991, *NJCM-Bulletin* 1991, p. 531, RSV 1992, p. 75.

6. ENFORCEMENT OF THE PRINCIPLE

6.1 COURT OR TRIBUNAL PROCEDURE

6.1.1 ACQUIRING THE EVIDENCE

6.1.1.1 Prescribed forms

The forms prescribed for presenting evidence in legal proceedings are provided for in the *Wetboek van Burgerlijke Rechtsvordering* (Civil Procedure Code). The relevant part of this Code has recently been amended (1 April 1988) to keep it up to date with changes brought about by case law. Article 179 of the Code provides that evidence may be presented by any means, unless the law provides otherwise. There are special rules for evidence by certificate or by witness. The weight to be attached to the evidence is, unless the law provides otherwise, a matter for the judge.

6.1.1.2 Obligation to furnish all relevant evidence

There is no obligation to furnish all relevant evidence. Since the burden of proof may be divided, the party who has to furnish evidence has to furnish sufficient evidence to satisfy the judge.

6.1.1.3 Annual information to works councils

An obligation to furnish annual information to the works council arises out of arts 28(3) and 31 of the Works Council Act. Article 28(3) requires the works council to guard against discrimination in the enterprise, and especially to promote equal opportunities for men and women. Article 31 requires the employer, if asked, to furnish the works council and its committees in good time with all information and data which they may reasonably need for carrying out their duties. The second paragraph enumerates a number of issues about which the employer has to give annual information to the works council, whether the council has asked for it or not. Information about equal treatment, the position of women in the enterprise and related matters are not among the subjects mentioned in that provision.

Article 31b of the Works Council Act may offer another method of obtaining information on this point. This provision obliges the employer to furnish annual written information concerning the numbers and the different groups of persons working in the enterprise, and concerning the social policy pursued in relation to them, especially in relation to those matters mentioned in arts 27, 28 and 29 of the Works Council Act.

6.1.1.4 Information to trade unions for bargaining

There is no formal obligation on the employer to furnish the trade unions with information for bargaining purposes. Such an obligation, however, can be included in a collective agreement. There are no figures available to indicate whether this happens in practice.

6.1.2 BURDEN OF PROOF

The principal rule about the burden of proof is laid down in art. 177 of the *Wetboek van Burgerlijke Rechtsvordering*, revised in 1988, which provides as follows:

> Anyone who claims the legal consequences of facts or rights has to prove those facts or rights, unless a different distribution of the burden of proof follows from a special rule or from the demands of reason and fairness.

This rule is not materially different from that previously in force. The case law under the former rule provided some clarification as to what this meant for the judge in distributing the burden of proof. In the *Binderen/Kaya* case,[1] which concerned racial discrimination, the *Hoge Raad* held that there is no rule of law to prevent the judge from considering numerical or statistical differences as a sufficient basis for a finding of discrimination, nor from using differences such as these as *prima facie* evidence and, solely on the basis of that evidence, from laying the burden of justifying the disadvantage on the party accused of discrimination. In two other cases the *Hoge Raad* ruled that there may be circumstances which would justify the normal burden of proof being alleviated by placing the other party under the obligation to furnish facts and data in order to help the claimant in his arguments.[2]

In social security cases the civil rule of burden of proof is not applicable. The *Algemene Wet Bestuursrecht* (General Act on Administrative Law), which contains no rules about evidence, provides for the role and jurisdiction of the judge. The judge in cases like these, unlike the judge in civil cases, is not passive; rather he has a broad freedom in the evaluation of the evidence. It is the judge who orders an examination if the facts in his view are insufficiently clear. Although the *Algemene Wet Bestuursrecht* does not explicitly put the burden of proof on either of the parties, the claimant must, pursuant to art. 6:5(1)(d), state the grounds on which his claim is founded. Although in practice the requirements for this are not strict, the claimant must show that there is a plausible basis for instituting an examination.

It is the opinion of the *Sociaal-economische Raad* that the rules laid down in the legislation and the accompanying case law probably more or less

---

1   HR, 10 December 1982, NJ 1983, 687.
2   HR, 11 December 1987, NJ 1988, 339, and HR, 20 November 1987, NJ 1988, 500.

reflect the intentions contained in the draft EC Directive on the burden of proof.[1]

6.1.3 COSTS

Proceedings before the Equal Treatment Committee are free of charge. For proceedings before the *Kantonrechter* and the courts the normal costs are a sum of Hfl 65 to Hfl 115, depending on the compensation claimed in the proceedings. The normal costs for proceedings before district courts are a sum of Hfl 250 to Hfl 300 for claims not exceeding Hfl 25,000, and 1.6 per cent of the sum of the claim, not exceeding Hfl 5,000 for the claimant and Hfl 1,200 for the defendant, when the sum claimed exceeds Hfl 25,000 (art. 11 of the *Wet Tarieven Burgerlijke Zaken*: Civil Procedure Costs Act). The normal costs for proceedings before the *Gerechtshof* (Regional Courts) and the *Hoge Raad* (Supreme Court) are Hfl 300 to 400 or 2 per cent of the sum claimed, up to a maximum of Hfl 6,250 for the claimant and Hfl 1,200 for the defendant.

The unsuccessful party will be ordered to pay the costs. The judge may order costs to be paid by both parties in appropriate cases;[2] this risk may act as a serious deterrent for potential litigants. The costs of court proceedings in social security cases are Hfl 50 for proceedings in the District Court (*Rechtbank*) and Hfl 150 for proceedings before the *Centrale Raad van Beroep*.

6.1.4 LEGAL AID

On 1 January 1994 the Act on Legal Aid for Persons with Insufficient Income (WROM: *Wet Rechtsbijstand On- en Minvermogenden*) was replaced by a new Legal Aid Act (*Wet op de Rechtsbijstand*). The WROM was originally introduced to remedy a situation in which legal aid was difficult to obtain for people with low incomes, and to overcome a shortage of specialists within the legal profession in areas such as labour law and social security law. It thus provided for subsidized legal aid, and solicitors assisting persons with incomes below a certain threshold could claim their fees from the state. The clients were to pay a small contribution, the level of which depended on their means. The WROM was very successful, so the expenses rose. An attempt was made to contain costs by raising clients' contributions while leaving solicitors' fees unchanged. The new Act worsens the situation quite dramatically. The main changes are the establishment of new Councils for Legal Aid, a reduction of the threshold for legal aid for single persons from Hfl 2,725 to Hfl 2,030 per month (the threshold for married persons remaining Hfl 2,980 per month),[3] a considerable increase in contributions

---

1   SER-*advies* 89/22, *Advies bewijslast gelijke behandeling vrouwen en mannen*, 's-Gravenhage, 1989.

2   Article 56 of the *Wetboek van Burgerlijke Rechtsvordering*.

3   Figures as at 1 January 1994.

and the restriction of legal aid to certain categories of cases. The Councils may decide not to grant legal aid if they do not consider a case to be of sufficient importance. Furthermore, fees will be paid to the solicitors in fewer cases. On the other hand they will be higher and index-linked.

6.1.5   REMEDIES

6.1.5.1   Nullity

An order of nullity is not unusual in labour law. For instance, dismissal without the prior permission of the director of a regional labour exchange is null and void, as is dismissal during pregnancy.

In equal treatment law an order of nullity may be made in relation to decisions or actions which are in breach of the obligation of the employer or the public authority to make no distinction between men and women in hiring, in labour conditions and in dismissal.[1] Discriminatory dismissals are null and void under article 8 of the *Algemene Wet Gelijke Behandeling* (General Equal Treatment Act). A dismissal because the dismissed person brought a claim, judicially or extra-judicially, under the equal treatment rule is null and void.[2]

6.1.5.2   Termination of discriminatory conduct

See §6.1.5.3 below.

6.1.5.3   Declaration

A litigant may always request a declaration that a certain act is unlawful, or an order by the judge requiring the other party to terminate the discriminatory conduct in question.

A different kind of declaration is available following an investigation, instituted at the request of the Minister for Social Affairs and Employment, under art. 21 of the Equal Treatment Act. If in that investigation it becomes clear that there is or has been discrimination within art. 1637ij of the Civil Code or the Equal Treatment Act, the Minister may inform the person responsible for the discrimination, as well as the works council, the employers' association, the trade union or organization of professionals, of the fact that discrimination occurred.

6.1.5.4   Compensation

Compensation seems to be the only available remedy in a number of cases of breach of the equal treatment law. When unequal treatment occurs in recruitment it is not clear how compensation is to be calculated. It may be,

---

1   Article 1637ij(7) of the Civil Code.
2   Article 1637ij(6) of the Civil Code.

however, that the merely symbolic compensation of Hfl 1 which the *Kantonrechter* awarded in a case where a woman was not hired for discriminatory reasons[1] does not meet the standards laid down by the ECJ in the *Harz* case.[2]

When the unequal treatment takes place in the course of the contract of employment, the unlawful conduct may be considered to be a breach of the obligations under the contract of employment, into which an equal treatment clause may be implied. The remedy for breach of contract is termination of the contract and/or compensation. In such cases the compensation may be the extra remuneration which has to be paid under the equal pay rule.

6.1.5.5   Recommendation

There are no special provisions in Dutch law. See also §6.1.5.6 below.

6.1.5.6   Positive enforceable order

Positive enforceable orders, for instance an order to select somebody for employment, have until now not been made as a remedy for breach of the equal treatment rule.

6.1.5.7   Positive action plan

Positive action plans have until now not been ordered by the courts to remedy unequal treatment, nor has this happened in cases concerning racial discrimination. In the parliamentary papers accompanying the amendment of the Equal Treatment Act the Minister stated:

> By including the possibility that an organization with full legal capacity may claim enforcement of the law before the courts when there has been or there is unequal treatment in relation to the field of application of the Act, the possibility arises that the claimant may for instance claim in court the institution of a positive action plan. Of course the claim and the cause of the procedure should be related: that is to say a positive action plan should include measures which may remove the breach of the law within a clearly defined time limit.[3]

---

1   *Kantongerecht* Gouda, 13 March 1986, *Praktijkgids*, 1987, p. 212.
2   *Harz* v. *Deutsche Tradax GmbH*, Case 79/83, [1984] ECR 1921 (ECJ).
3   TK 19 908, 6, p. 11.

6.1.5.8 Correction

When the breach of the equal treatment rule consists of an unlawful advertisement the Court may order the publication of a correction.[1]

6.1.6 CLASS ACTIONS

The right to bring a class action was included in the original provisions of the Equal Treatment Act. This right has been extended with the amendment of the Equal Treatment Act of 1 July 1989 in two ways. The first is that the works council now also has the right to ask for the Equal Treatment Committee's opinion about equal treatment in the enterprise (for the current position see art. 12 of the General Equal Treatment Act). The works council is not, however, competent to start legal proceedings before the courts. The second is that the right of a body corporate, enjoying full legal capacity, to institute proceedings has been extended. The organization cannot claim compensation for itself, but may claim damages on behalf of an individual. The organization may also ask the Equal Treatment Committee for an opinion; this right exists regardless of the question as to whether or not the injured individual himself has the right to file a claim. It is not possible, however, for the organization to start court proceedings if the person concerned objects; nor can the Equal Treatment Committee institute an investigation if the injured person objects.

The right of an organization to take action to enforce the Equal Treatment Act is perhaps the most important change yet made to the Act, as individuals may be reluctant to take proceedings against their employer.

There are a number of organizations in the Netherlands in the field of human rights in general and equal opportunities in particular. They may actively participate in the enforcement of the equal treatment rule.

Since 1994 class actions are provided for in art. 3:305a of the Civil Code.[2]

6.1.7 EXCLUSION OF JUDICIAL REDRESS

Exclusion of judicial redress is declared unconstitutional by art. 17 of the Dutch Constitution, which reads:

Nobody may against his will be obstructed from access to a court made available by law.

6.1.8 TIME LIMITS

Time limits in equal treatment law are prescribed by the Equal Treatment Act and the Civil Code. The first set of time limits concerns the

---

[1] Article 3(5) of the Equal Treatment Act.
[2] Stb 1994, 269.

barring of equal pay actions by lapse of time. A pay claim is normally barred after five years.[1] Claims for equal pay under the Equal Treatment Act, however, are barred after two years.[2] It is possible for the claimant to prevent the lapse of time resulting in the barring of a claim by starting proceedings through taking measures such as applying for a subpoena or summons. An application for an opinion by the Equal Treatment Committee is not considered to be sufficient. The difference between the normal time limit and this shorter time limit was justified by the complexity of equal pay cases by the Minister in introducing the Equal Pay Act 1975, in which this provision was included.

The second set of time limits concerns the annulment of a dismissal. An employer is not allowed to dismiss an employee in a discriminatory way or because the employee invoked a provision of equal treatment law. Such a dismissal is null and void. The annulment of the dismissal must be sought by the employee within two months after the dismissal. Claims by the employee resulting from this nullity (not being compensation), e.g. continued pay, are barred after six months.[3]

The third set of time limits concerns claims for compensation. Here the normal time limits are applicable, by which claims are barred after 20 years.[4] If the claims for compensation are under art. 1639s of the Civil Code (apparently unreasonable dismissal, in cases where the claim is instituted because of discriminatory dismissal), the claim is barred after six months.[5]

6.2   COURTS AND TRIBUNALS

Courts and tribunals may hear cases concerning equal treatment. If the case concerns a contract of employment, the *Kantonrechter* is competent, whatever the amount of the claim. If the case concerns a civil servant, the *Ambtenarenrechter* is competent.

6.2.1   SPECIAL COURT OR TRIBUNAL

Labour courts as such are unknown in the Netherlands. All civil disputes connected with a contract of employment or a collective agreement come under the jurisdiction of the ordinary courts, the *Kantongerechten* that are competent, generally, for small claims, and for any claim concerning a labour contract or concerning rent. In social security cases, special chambers of the *Rechtbanken* (District Courts) are competent.

---

1   Article 3:308 of the Civil Code.
2   Article 11 of the Equal Treatment Act.
3   Article 1637ij(6) of the Civil Code and art. la(6) of the Equal Treatment Act.
4   Article 3:306 of the Civil Code.
5   Article 1639u of the Civil Code.

The ordinary courts are:

(a) the (62) Lower Courts (*Kantonrechter*)
(b) the (19) District Courts (*Arrondissementsrechtbank* or *Rechtbank*)
(c) the (5) Courts of Appeal (*Gerechtshof*)
(d) the Supreme Court (*Hoge Raad*).

A decision of the Lower Court judge is generally subject to appeal in a District Court. The District Court has a general jurisdiction of first instance over all major offences and for civil cases which have not been allocated to the Lower Court. A decision of a District Court is subject to the appellate jurisdiction of the Court of Appeal.

The decisions of Lower Courts, District Courts and the Court of Appeal are subject to an appeal to the Supreme Court; in such cases the Court is bound by the facts as found in the lower courts and has jurisdiction only to rule on questions of law.

6.2.1.1 Equality officer

This institution does not exist in the Netherlands.

6.2.1.2 Arbitration court

The right to arbitration is not important in the context of this work. Some collective agreements provide for the settlement through arbitration of disputes arising from the agreement. An example of this is a case decided by the *Centrale Commissie voor het administratief personeel in het Dagbladbedrijf* (Central committee for clerical personnel in newspaper companies) on 6 December 1978.[1]

6.2.1.3 Equal opportunities agency

The Equal Treatment Act set up an independent Equal Treatment Committee, consisting of experts, to further the implementation of equal treatment law. The members are experts in the sense that they have sufficient knowledge and experience in the field of the legislation. This Committee of experts delivers an opinion on whether in a specific case or in the case of a specific regulation there is a breach of the law. The opinion has neither the force of legally binding advice, nor may it be treated as a judicial decision; it is up to the parties to the case to act in response to it.

The aim of this institutional framework is to avoid the use of judicial procedures and to facilitate solutions in cases where discrimination has taken place, not because of discriminatory intent, but because of ignorance of the

---

[1]   GERRITSEN I, p. 116

relevant law. In such circumstances voluntary procedures may be preferable. Furthermore, the procedures whereby the Committee gives its opinion are free of charge and may be instituted in a very simple way.[1]

Since 1 September 1994, the Equal Treatment Committee has been regulated by the *Algemene Wet Gelijke Behandeling* (General Equal Treatment Act). The tasks of the Equal Treatment Committee concern equal treatment not only in the field of sex discrimination, but in other fields as well.

6.2.1.4 *Regionaal Directeur voor de Arbeidsvoorziening* (Regional Labour Exchange Director)

Pursuant to art. 6 of the *Buitengewoon Besluit Arbeidsverhoudingen* 1945 (Labour Relations (Special Power) Decree) no employment relationship may be terminated without the consent of the Minister for Social Affairs, who delegates this authority to the director of the regional labour exchange. In deciding whether to grant his consent, the director may take into account whether the termination of the labour relationship is discriminatory, and in violation of the equal treatment principle. When an opinion of the Equal Treatment Committee has been requested, the director does not wait for that opinion before taking a decision about consent for termination of the labour relation.

6.2.2   SPECIALIZED TRAINING FOR JUDGES

Occasionally, specialized training relevant to this topic, in the form of one or two-day courses, are organized by the *Stichting Studiecentrum Rechtspleging*, the Foundation which is generally entrusted with training for judges.

6.2.3   SPECIALIZATION WITHIN THE SYSTEM

There are no signs that specialization is taking place within the judicial system. Considering the small number of cases, this is not surprising.

6.3   ENFORCEMENT AGENCY

6.3.1   TYPE

6.3.1.1   Labour inspectorate

The Labour Inspectorate is a Government body, charged with controlling the observance of a number of labour statutes. The Labour Inspectorate does not, however, have an explicit role in relation to the

---

[1]   TK 19 908, 3, p. 7.

enforcement of the Equal Treatment Act. Here the Minister for Social Affairs and Employment is competent to institute an investigation by officers to be designated by him. Usually these will be officers of the *Loontechnische Dienst* (Service for technical wage matters), a department of the Ministry of Social Affairs which has also been appointed to assist the Equal Treatment Committee in the performance of its task.

6.3.1.2   Equal opportunities agency

The tasks of an equal opportunities agency have in the Netherlands been distributed among three different bodies, the *Emancipatieraad* (Emancipation Council), the *Commissie Vrouw en Arbeid* of the *Sociaal-economische Raad* (Committee on women and work of the Social and Economic Council) and the Equal Treatment Committee.

Both the *Emancipatieraad* and the *Sociaal-economische Raad* are independent advisory bodies. The *Emancipatieraad* has to advise the Government on matters where the position of men and women in society is at issue. The *Raad* consists of 11 members, appointed for their expertise.

The *Sociaal-economische Raad* advises the Government about issues of a social or economic nature. It is the most important advisory body in this field. Membership consists of 15 representatives from trade unions, 15 representatives from employers' organizations and 15 independent members appointed by the Crown.

The Equal Treatment Committee is an autonomous body. Its nine members, including the President, and their deputies are appointed by the Minister for Justice, in agreement with the Ministers for Internal Affairs, for Social Affairs, for Education and for Welfare. For appointment, expertise and experience are decisive. Expertise and experience in this context mean legal expertise and experience of one or more grounds of discrimination and one or more of the types of discrimination covered by the Act.

6.3.2   FUNCTIONS

6.3.2.1   Advice

The task of advising the Government on equal opportunities matters rests explicitly with the *Emancipatieraad*. Because equal opportunities matters are part of general social and economic policy, the *Sociaal-economische Raad* and the *Commissie Vrouw en Arbeid* also advise the Government in this field.

The Equal Treatment Committee, although not formally entrusted with this duty, has in the past also submitted advice to the Minister on a number of occasions, for instance on the amendment of the Equal Treatment Act.

6.3.2.2 Research

None of the bodies mentioned here is entrusted with the duty to undertake research on equal opportunities matters. However, the Equal Treatment Committee can commission research.

6.3.2.3 Legal aid

None of the bodies mentioned here provides legal aid. For legal aid, a special organization of the Bar is responsible. Legal aid is also given by trade unions and by institutions such as the *Ombudsvrouw* (private organizations which are concerned with the position of women).

6.3.3 REMEDIES

6.3.3.1 Notice

The Equal Treatment Committee can, upon written request or of its own accord, investigate whether discrimination as defined by the General Equal Treatment Act has been committed, and make its opinion known. The Committee's opinion is brought to the attention of the person who asked for it, and also to the attention of the person who is deemed to have committed the discrimination, by written and reasoned notice.

The Committee may also inform the Ministers concerned, the employers' organizations, the trade unions and the works council of the notice. In the case of an opinion on the question whether in offering a job there has been discrimination, the Committee may publicize this opinion or an excerpt in whatever way it thinks appropriate.[1]

6.3.3.2 Injunction

The Committee may file a claim before the Court that an act that is in violation of the General Equal Treatment Act, the Equal Treatment Act or article 1637ij of the Civil Code be declared unlawful, that that act is forbidden or that an order be issued that the consequences of that act be undone.

6.3.3.3 Compensation

The Equal Treatment Committee does not have the power to order the payment of compensation.

---

[1] Articles 12 and 13 of the General Equal Treatment Act.

6.4   COLLECTIVE AGREEMENTS

6.4.1   EQUAL PAY CLAUSE

No express equal pay clauses are to be found in collective agreements. They might, however, be considered by implication to be part of collective agreements.[1] In a number of collective agreements, however, there are clauses which might be considered to be part of a positive action plan.[2]

6.4.2   AUTOMATIC NULLITY

The Collective Agreements (Pronouncement of Binding and Non-binding Provisions) Act 1937 (AVV)[3] declares null and void any provision in an individual contract of employment contrary to a provision in the collective agreement.

6.4.3   COLLECTIVE REDRESS

If the equal treatment principle is incorporated into a collective agreement, the trade unions and the employers' associations may themselves claim compensation for damages suffered by breach of the equal treatment or equal pay principle, either by the party to the collective agreement, or by an individual employer. Pursuant to art. 15 of the Collective Agreements (Pronouncement of Binding and Non-binding Provisions) Act the damages may relate to both the damage suffered by the members of the trade union and by the association itself. However, no instances are known where this has been applied.

6.4.4   AGENCY MONITORING

There is no relevant law in the Netherlands on this point.

6.4.5   CONTRACT COMPLIANCE

No contract compliance procedures are, as yet, to be found in the Netherlands.

---

1   See I.P. ASSCHER-VONK, 'Vorderingen tot naleving van de Wet gelijke behandeling van mannen en vrouwen', SMA 1980, p. 503, especially p. 511.

2   Ministerie van Sociale Zaken en Werkgelegenheid, *Aspecten van emancipatie in CAO's*, 's-Gravenhage, January 1988.

3   *Wet op het Algemeen Verbindend en Onverbindend Verklaren van Bepalingen van Collectieve Arbeidsovereenkomsten.*

SOURCES OF
EQUALITY LAW

7. LEGISLATION

7.1   CONSTITUTIONAL PROVISIONS ON EQUALITY

CONSTITUTION OF THE KINGDOM OF THE NETHERLANDS [1]

Article 1

All persons on Dutch territory are treated equally in the same circumstances. Discrimination on the grounds of religion, creed, political faith, race, sex or on any other ground is not permitted.

Article 3

All Dutch persons are equally eligible for public service.

7.2   LIST OF NATIONAL ACTS RATIFYING INTERNATIONAL TREATIES IN MATTERS OF EQUALITY

(a) Universal Declaration of Human Rights;[2] this is not a treaty *stricto sensu*. Ratification is not required;

(b) Act of 28 July 1954[3] ratifying the European Convention for the Protection of Human Rights and Fundamental Freedoms;[4]

(c) Act of 23 April 1971 ratifying the Equal Remuneration Convention;[5]

(d) Act of 5 December 1957 ratifying the EEC Treaty;[6]

(e) Act of 4 December 1972 ratifying the Discrimination (Employment and Occupation) Convention;[7]

(f) Act of 2 November 1978 ratifying the European Social Charter;[8]

---

[1] 24 August 1815, Stb 1815, 45, last revised 17 February 1983, Stb 1983, 70.

[2] 10 December 1948.

[3] Stb 1954, 335.

[4] 4 November 1950, Rome. The Protocols were ratified on the following dates: First Protocol: 31 August 1954; Second Protocol: 4 September 1966; Third Protocol: 4 September 1966; Fourth Protocol: 10 March 1982; Fifth Protocol: 20 December 1971.

[5] ILO Convention No 100 of 29 June 1951. The question of direct effect for ILO Conventions in the Netherlands is not clear: see A.T.J.M. JACOBS, *De rechtstreekse werking van internationale normen in het sociaal recht,* Alphen aan den Rijn, 1985, p. 22.

[6] Stb 1957, 493.

[7] ILO Convention No 111 of 25 June 1958.

[8] Stb 1978, 639.

(g) Act of 18 February 1971 ratifying the International Covenant on the Elimination of All Forms of Racial Discrimination;[1]

(h) Act of 24 November 1978 ratifying the International Covenant on Economic, Social and Cultural Rights;[2]

(i) Act of 24 November 1978 ratifying the International Covenant on Civil and Political Rights.[3]

(j) Act of 3 July 1991 ratifying the Convention on the Elimination of All Forms of Discrimination against Women.[4]

7.3   NATIONAL TEXTS CONTAINING GENERAL PROVISIONS ON EQUALITY: ACTS

7.3.1   COLLECTIVE AGREEMENTS ACT (ACT OF 24 DECEMBER 1927)[5]

Article 1

(...)

(3) Any stipulation, requiring the employer not to employ or exclusively to employ employees of a specific race, a specific religious denomination or political persuasion or members of a specific association, is null and void.

7.3.2   COLLECTIVE AGREEMENTS (PRONOUNCEMENT OF BINDING AND NON-BINDING PROVISIONS) ACT (ACT OF 25 MAY 1937)[6]

Article 2

(...)

(5) A declaration as to its binding effect shall not be made in respect of the provisions of a collective agreement designed to:

(...)

(c) bring about the unequal treatment of organized and unorganized members of the workforce.

---

1   Stb 1971, 76.
2   Stb 1978, 624.
3   Stb 1978, 624. In a number of cases art. 26 of the International Covenant on Civil and Political Rights has been applied by the courts in cases of discrimination between men and women which took place before Directive 79/7/EEC took effect, in cases of discrimination between men and women not covered by the Directive (widowers' pensions), and in cases where there was discrimination on other grounds (for instance between married and cohabiting couples).
4   Stb 1991, 355.
5   Stb 1927, 415.
6   Stb 1937, 801.

7.3.3 PENAL CODE

Article 429 *quater* [1]

(1) Any person who in exercising a profession or a trade discriminates between persons on the ground of race is punishable by imprisonment not exceeding one month or a fine in the third category.

(2) This provision shall not apply to actions which grant preferential treatment to persons belonging to certain ethnic or cultural minorities.

7.3.4 WORKS COUNCIL ACT (ACT OF 28 JANUARY 1971)[2]

Article 28

(...)

(3) A works council shall guard against discrimination in the undertaking and shall in particular encourage the equal treatment of men and women in the undertaking and the employment of handicapped workers.

7.3.5 CIVIL CODE

Article 3:305a[3]

(1) A foundation or body corporate enjoying full legal capacity may file a claim for the protection of interests of third parties, provided that those interests are compatible with its statute.

(2) A legal person within the terms of paragraph (1) cannot institute proceedings if it has not in the circumstances sufficiently consulted with the defendant with a view to reaching a settlement of the claim.

(3) A claim covered by paragraph (1) may not give rise to pecuniary damages.

(4) A claim covered by paragraph (1) cannot be founded upon an act, if the person prejudiced by that act objects to the claim.

(5) A judgment shall not apply to a person in whose interests a claim is made if that person resists the effect of the judgment, unless the character of the judgment is such that its effect cannot be excluded for one person.

---

[1]   Article introduced in 1971.
[2]   Stb 1971, 54.
[3]   Article introduced 1 July 1994.

Article 1639h [1]

(...)

(2)   An employer shall not be entitled to give notice of termination of employment to an employee because of the employee's marriage.

(...)

(4)   An employer shall not be entitled to give notice of termination of employment to a worker who is fit to perform the agreed work during pregnancy and because of her confinement.

An employer shall be entitled to demand a statement for confirmation of the pregnancy from a physician or a midwife. Furthermore the employer shall not be entitled to give notice to a worker who resumed work after the confinement for a period from the seventh until the eleventh week after confinement.

...

7.3.6   GENERAL EQUAL TREATMENT ACT (ACT OF 2 MARCH 1994) [2]

Article 8

(1)   Termination of an employment relationship by the employer in contravention of article 5,[3] or because the employee has filed a judicial or extra-judicial claim under article 5, is null and void.

(2)   Notwithstanding the provisions of the *Ambtenarenwet 1929* (Civil Servants Act 1929), the employee may, within two months after notice has been given or after the termination of the employment relationship by the employer otherwise than by giving notice, claim the nullity of a termination in the circumstances described in paragraph (1). Nullity shall be claimed by notice to the employer. Termination in the circumstances described in paragraph (1) shall not render the employer liable to damages. Every claim for nullity of a termination under the provisions of this paragraph shall be barred after the lapse of six months.

...

Chapter II
The Equal Treatment Committee

Article 11

(1)   There is hereby established an Equal Treatment Committee, hereafter referred to as the Committee.

(2) The Committee may form chambers for the fulfilment of its task.

---

1   Article introduced 1 August 1976.
2   Stb 1994, 230.
3   Article 5 of the General Equal Treatment Act forbids, *inter alia*, discrimination in dismissal.

Article 12

(1) The Committee may, upon a written application, institute an inquiry into whether there is or has been discrimination which is covered by this Act, the Equal Treatment Act (Men and Women) or article 1637ij of the Civil Code, and make known its opinion on the matter. Moreover, the Committee may of its own accord institute an inquiry into whether such discrimination occurs systematically in the civil service or in one or more sectors of society, and make its opinion upon the matter known.

(2) A written application of the kind referred to in the first paragraph can be made by:

(a) any person considering that there is or has been discrimination to their detriment covered by this Act, the Equal Treatment Act (Men and Women) or article 1637ij of the Civil Code;

(b) a natural person, legal person or competent authority wishing to know whether they are committing a discrimination covered by this Act, the Equal Treatment Act (Men and Women) or article 1637ij of the Civil Code;

(c) the person responsible for determining a dispute concerning discrimination covered by this Act, the Equal Treatment Act (Men and Women) or article 1637ij of the Civil Code;

(d) a works council which takes the view that in the undertaking for which it has been established, or the committee covered by Chapter XIA of the *Algemeen Rijksambtenarenreglement* (Regulation on civil servants) or a similar regulation, which takes the view that in a certain department for which it is established, a discrimination covered by this Act, the Equal Treatment Act (Men and Women) or article 1637ij of the Civil Code is being committed;

(e) a legal person with full legal capacity which in accordance with its regulations promotes the interests of persons for whose protection this Act, the Equal Treatment Act (Men and Women) or article 1637ij of the Civil Code aims to provide.

(3) If a written application covered by subparagraphs 2(d) and 2(e) mentions persons who have been treated in a detrimental manner, or if an inquiry of the Committee's own accord refers to such persons, the Committee shall inform these persons of its intention to institute an inquiry. The Committee may not involve in the inquiry and the opinion those persons referred to in the first sentence who have declared in writing that they object.

Article 13

(1) The Committee shall institute an inquiry and inform the applicant and the person alleged to have committed the discrimination and, as the case may be, the person against whom the discrimination might have been committed, of its opinion in writing, together with its reasons.

(2) When informing the person who is alleged to have committed the discrimination, the Committee may make recommendations.

(3)   The Committee may give notice of its opinion to Our Ministers whom it concerns, and to such employers' organizations, workers' organizations, organizations concerned with professional life or with civil servants, organizations of consumers of goods and services and consultative bodies as are concerned in the matter.

Article 14

(1)   The Committee will not institute an inquiry if:
(a) the application covered by article 12, paragraph (2) appears to be groundless;
(b) the interest of the applicant or the gravity of the act appears to be insufficient;
(c) since the discrimination covered by article 12 too much time has expired to make an effective inquiry reasonably possible.

(2)   If cases covered by the first paragraph occur, the Committee will give a written and reasoned notice thereof to the applicant.

Article 15

(1)   The Committee may file a claim before the Court that an act that is in violation of this Act, the Equal Treatment Act (Men and Women) or article 1637ij of the Civil Code be declared unlawful, that that act is forbidden or that an order be issued that the consequences of that act be undone.

(2)   A claim covered by the first paragraph cannot be founded upon an act, if the person prejudiced by that act objects to the claim.

Article 16

(1)   The Committee shall consist of nine members, including the president and two vice-presidents, and an equal number of deputies.

(2)   The president and the vice-presidents shall meet the qualifications for appointment as a judge of a District Court set out in article 48, paragraph (1) of the Act for Judicial Organization.

(3)   The members and their deputies are appointed by Our Minister for Justice, in agreement with Our Minister for Internal Affairs, Our Minister for Social Affairs and Employment, Our Minister for Education and Science and Our Minister for Welfare, Public Health and Culture.

(....)

(5)   When applying article 14d, paragraph (2) of the Act for Judicial Organization, the Supreme Court will enable the president of the Committee to give information either orally or in writing about any complaint which may be pending and to make the president's views thereon known.

(6)   The members and their deputies will hold office for a maximum period of six years. They may be directly reappointed. The Minister for Justice may dismiss them if they so request.

Article 17

(1) The Committee is supported by a bureau.

(2) Our Minister for Justice appoints to the bureau, promotes, suspends and dismisses its officers, on the recommendation of the Committee.

(3) The secretary, who shall also be head of the bureau, shall meet the qualifications for appointment as a judge of a District Court set out in article 48, paragraph (1) of the Act for Judicial Organization.

Article 18

(1) The Committee may be assisted in the performance of its task by civil servants designated for that purpose by Our Minister whom it concerns.

(2) The Committee may, in the performance of its task, seek assistance from any person or persons in order to procure information necessary for the fulfilment of its work.

(3) The members refrain from participation in an inquiry if there are facts or circumstances that may be prejudicial to their impartiality.

Article 19

(1) The Committee and the persons referred to in article 17 who are designated by the Committee may request any information and documents which are reasonably required for the performance of its task.

(2) Any person required to supply information and documents must do so completely and truthfully, in the manner prescribed and within the time-limit set by or on behalf of the Committee, without prejudice to their right to refuse to reply on grounds of professional secrecy. This obligation does not apply if a person by doing so would lay either themselves or one of their relatives, their spouse or former spouse open to conviction for a criminal offence.

Article 20

(1) The Committee shall issue an annual report of its activity and publish that report. It shall send this report to the Ministers and the advisory bodies which it concerns.

(2) After every period of five years counting from the date upon which this Act comes into effect the Committee shall draw up a report on its findings concerning the effect in practice of this Act, the Equal Treatment Act (Men and Women) and article 1637ij of the Civil Code. It will send the report to the Minister for Internal Affairs.

Article 21

(1) Further rules shall be prescribed by general government order concerning the working method of the Committee, including:
(a) procedures
(b) hearing of both parties
(c) proceedings in open court
(d) publication of opinions in terms of article 13, paragraph (3).

(2) The remuneration, travel and lodging allowances and other emoluments of the members of the Committee and their deputies will be prescribed by general government order. The unemployment benefits of the members of the Committee after the period of their appointment will be similarly prescribed.

Chapter III
Final provisions

Article 22

Any persons concerned with the application of this Act who in consequence have information in their possession of which they recognize or should recognize the confidential nature, and who are not already bound to secrecy by virtue of their office or occupation or by reason of a legal obligation, must keep that information secret, unless they are obliged by law to make it public or such publication stems from their role in the application of this Act.

...

Article 35

This Act may be cited as the General Equal Treatment Act.

7.4 NATIONAL TEXTS IMPLEMENTING EC DIRECTIVES: EQUAL PAY

7.4.1 EQUAL TREATMENT ACT (ACT OF 1 MARCH 1980): ACT TO HARMONIZE NETHERLANDS LEGISLATION WITH THE DIRECTIVE OF THE COUNCIL OF THE EUROPEAN COMMUNITIES OF 9 FEBRUARY 1976 ON EQUAL TREATMENT FOR MEN AND WOMEN,[1] AS AMENDED ON 1 JULY 1989[2]

Chapter I
Equal treatment of men and women in employment

[For Part 1 (arts 1-6) of Chapter I see §7.5.2 below]

Part 2: Equal pay for work of equal value

Article 7

(1) For the purposes of article 1637ij of the Civil Code, the basis for comparing the employment conditions referred to in that article shall be, in so far as wages are concerned, the wages normally enjoyed by a worker of the other sex for work of equal value or, in the absence of such work, for work of approximately equal value, in the undertaking where the worker on whose behalf the comparison is made is employed.

---

1   Stb 1980, 86.
2   Stb 1989, 168.

(2) The wages referred to in the first paragraph consist of the remuneration payable by an employer to a worker in return for the work, excluding benefits or entitlements under any pension scheme.

Article 8

For the purposes of article 7 work shall be assessed in accordance with a reliable system of job evaluation; to this end recourse shall be had as far as possible to the system customary in the undertaking where the worker concerned is employed. In the absence of such a system, the work shall be fairly assessed in the light of the available information.

Article 9

(1) For the purposes of article 7 the wages received by the worker concerned shall be deemed to be equal to the wage that a worker of the other sex normally receives for work of equal value if it is calculated on the basis of equivalent criteria.

(2) For the purposes of article 7 account shall be taken of elements of wages other than cash in accordance with the market value that can be assigned to them.

(3) Where a worker has agreed with an employer on hours of work which are shorter than those normally considered in corresponding employment relationships to represent full-time employment, the wage to which the worker would be entitled if in full-time employment shall be proportionately reduced in so far as it is calculated on the basis of a unit of time.

Article 10

Further provisions relating to the matters covered by articles 7, 8 and 9 may be made in regulations.

Article 11

The right to claim payment of wages under this Act shall be barred by limitation after two years have expired since payment should have been made. Article 2013 of the Civil Code shall apply, *mutatis mutandis*, to the period of limitation.

Article 12

For the purposes of articles 1a and 1b this Part of Chapter 1 is equally applicable.

[For subsequent articles see §7.5.2 below]

7.5   NATIONAL TEXTS IMPLEMENTING EC DIRECTIVES: EQUAL TREATMENT

7.5.1   CIVIL CODE

Article 1637ij

(1) An employer shall not make any distinction between men and women when entering into a contract of employment, providing training for a worker, determining his conditions of employment, deciding on his promotion or terminating his contract of employment. The expression 'conditions of employment' does not include benefits or claims under any pension scheme.

(2) A departure from the provision laid down in the first sentence of the first paragraph of this article shall be permitted only for the purposes of entering into a contract of employment and providing training in cases where a person's sex constitutes a determining factor. Article 5(3) of the Equal Treatment Act shall similarly apply.

(3) A departure from the provision laid down in the first sentence of the first paragraph of this article shall be permitted if it concerns stipulations relating to protection for women, and particularly pregnancy or maternity.

(4) A departure from the provision laid down in the first sentence of the first paragraph shall be permitted if it concerns stipulations designed to place women in a privileged position in order to remove existing inequalities.

(5) In this article references to a distinction between men and women shall include direct and indirect discrimination between men and women.

Direct discrimination includes a distinction on the ground of pregnancy, confinement and maternity. Indirect discrimination means a distinction on the ground of qualities other than sex, for instance marital status or family circumstances, which results in discrimination on the ground of sex. The prohibition of distinctions imposed by the first paragraph of this article does not apply to distinctions which are objectively justified.

(6) An employer's termination of an employment relationship where the worker has lodged a complaint, either judicially or extra-judicially, under the provisions of the first paragraph of this article, shall be null and void. The worker shall be entitled to claim that termination a nullity for a period of two months after he received notice, or for a period of two months after the employment relationship was terminated if the employer terminated it otherwise than by giving notice. Such nullity shall be claimed by means of a notification served on the employer. The employer shall not be liable for damages on account of his termination of the employment relationship referred to in the first sentence of this paragraph.

(7) Any stipulation contrary to the provisions of the first sentence of the first paragraph is null and void.

7.5.2   EQUAL TREATMENT ACT (ACT OF 1 MARCH 1980): ACT TO HARMONIZE NETHERLANDS LEGISLATION WITH THE DIRECTIVE OF THE COUNCIL OF THE EUROPEAN COMMUNITIES OF 9 FEBRUARY 1976 ON EQUAL TREATMENT FOR MEN AND WOMEN,[1] AS AMENDED ON 1 JULY 1989[2]

Chapter I
Equal treatment of men and women in employment

Part 1: General

Article 1

In this Act a distinction between men and women includes direct and indirect discrimination between men and women.

Direct discrimination includes a distinction on the ground of pregnancy, confinement and maternity. Indirect discrimination means a distinction on the ground of qualities other than sex, for instance marital status or family circumstances, which results in discrimination on the ground of sex.

Article 1a

(1)   In public service the competent authority shall not make any distinction between men and women in an appointment to a post of civil servant or an employment contract according to civil law, in determining conditions of employment, providing training for a worker, determining his conditions of employment, deciding on his promotion or terminating the employment relationship. The expression 'conditions of employment' does not include benefits or claims under any pension scheme.

(2)   All institutions, services and undertakings, administered by the State and the public bodies, are counted as public service.

(3)   Departure from the provision laid down in the first paragraph is permitted if it concerns protection for women, particularly in relation to pregnancy and maternity.

(4)   The competent authority may not terminate the employment of a person employed in the civil service because the person concerned has lodged a complaint, either judicially or extra-judicially, under the provisions of the first paragraph.

(5)   The termination contrary to this law of an employment relationship of a person who is employed in the civil service on a Civil Code employment contract will not make the authority liable for damages. In that case the person concerned shall be entitled to claim nullity within a period of two months after he received notice, or after the employment relationship was terminated if the competent authority has terminated it otherwise than by

---

1   Stb 1980, 86.
2   Stb 1989, 168.

giving notice. Such nullity shall be claimed by means of a notice served on the employer.

Every claim of the person concerned in connection with the annulment of the termination under this paragraph becomes barred after a lapse of six months.

(6) Any stipulation contrary to the provisions of the first sentence of the first paragraph is null and void.

Article 1b

If an individual, body corporate or the competent authority lets a person perform work in its service in any other way than under a contract of employment or as a civil servant, article 1637ij of the Civil Code is similarly applicable.

Article 2

It shall not be permissible to make any distinction between men and women, either directly or indirectly (e.g. by referring to their marital status or family circumstances), in connection with the conditions of access to, or the development opportunities and practice within, a liberal profession.

Article 3

(1) It shall not be permissible to make any distinction between men and women in offering employment or in the procedures followed for the purpose of filling a vacancy.

(2) Departure from the provisions of the first paragraph is permitted when, in accordance with this or any other Act, it is permitted to make a distinction between men and women, and if, in so far as it concerns the public advertising of employment, explicit mention is made of the reason for that discrimination.

(3) An offer of employment, under the first paragraph, should be made, both in text and through design, in such a way that it is clear that both men and women are considered for the vacancy.

(4) If a title is used for the job offered, both the male and female form of the title shall be used, or it should be mentioned expressly that both women and men are eligible for the vacancy.

(5) If any party is liable to a person for damages for an unlawful act on account of an employment offer in violation of the provisions of this Act, the judge can, if that person or a body corporate covered by article 20a has requested it, order the publication of a rectification in a manner indicated by the judge.

Article 4

(1) No individual or body corporate providing vocational training, advanced vocational training or courses for supplementary training or retraining, however styled, or an individual or body corporate holding an examination in connection with training or courses mentioned above shall, in relation to access to and treatment within the training or courses, or in holding the examination, make any distinction between men and women, whether in connection with criteria or in connection with standards.

(2) Departure from the provisions of the first paragraph is permitted, except for holding examinations and only if provisions of equal value are available for students of both sexes, where the particular nature of an institution providing special education constitutes an obstacle.

(3) Any stipulation contrary to the provisions of paragraph (1) of this article shall be null and void.

Article 5

(1) A departure from the provisions of articles 1a, 2, 3 and 4 is permitted where the distinction made is designed to place women in a privileged position in order to remove or reduce existing inequalities and the distinction is in reasonable proportion to the aim pursued.

(2) In so far as it concerns access to occupations and training necessary for that purpose, a departure from articles 1a, 2, 3 and 4 is permitted where because of the nature of or the conditions for the exercise of the occupation sex constitutes a determining factor.

(3) Only occupations which belong to or provide training for one or more of the following categories are considered to be ones for which, because of their nature or the conditions under which they are exercised, sex is a determining factor:
(a) ecclesiastical offices;
(b) the professional occupations of actor, actress, singer, dancer or artiste, in so far as these occupations are relevant to the interpretation of certain parts;
(c) other occupations, to be prescribed by Regulation.

Article 6

The prohibition of distinctions imposed by this Act does not apply to indirect discrimination which is objectively justified.

[For Part 2 (arts 7-12) of Chapter I, concerning equal pay, see §7.4.1 above.

Chapters II and III are repealed. The rules are now contained in the General Equal Treatment Act (see §7.3.6 above) and in art. 3:305a of the Civil Code (see §7.3.5 above).]

Chapter IV
Final provisions

Article 21

(1) Our Minister for Social Affairs and Employment may institute inquiries for the purposes of supervision of compliance with article 1637ij Civil Code and the provisions of this Act by officers designated by him. In so far as it concerns the civil service Our Minister for Internal Affairs may request Our Minister for Social Affairs and Employment to institute an inquiry covered by the first paragraph.

(2) If it appears from the inquiry that discrimination, covered by article 1637ij of the Civil Code or the provisions of this Act, is taking place Our Minister for Social Affairs and Employment shall communicate this to the person, the body corporate or the competent authority which has made the distinction or still makes the distinction and, if it concerns discrimination covered by article 1637ij of the Civil Code or article 1a or article 1b of this Act, to the Works Council concerned or to the Committee, covered by Chapter XIA of the *Algemeen Rijksambtenarenreglement* (General Regulation on Civil Servants) or by a similar regulation, and also to the employers' and workers' organizations, the professional organizations and the civil servants' organizations whom he considers qualified. The communication to the Works Council, to the Committee, covered by Chapter XIA of the *Algemeen Rijksambtenarenreglement* or by a similar regulation, and to these organizations, shall not contain details which may reveal the identity of the persons implicated in the inquiry, to the detriment of whom the distinction has been or is being made.

(3) The officers designated in the first paragraph may request all information and documents which within reason are needed for the accomplishment of their task.

(4) Any person who is requested by the Committee or the officer concerned to supply the information and documents designated in the third paragraph must do so completely and truthfully, without prejudice to the right to refuse answers because of professional confidentiality, as requested by and within the time limit set by the Committee or the officer concerned.

(...)

Article 23

The recommendation to amend a General Regulation pursuant to article 5(3)(c), and the recommendation for a General Regulation pursuant to article 10 is not made before the draft has been published in the *Nederlandse Staatscourant* and any person concerned therewith has had the opportunity to make representations to Our Minister within 30 days after the day the publication has been made. On the same day the draft shall be presented to Parliament.

Article 24

(1) This Act may be cited as the Equal Treatment Act (Men and Women).

(2) This Act shall come into operation on the second day following the date of publication of the *Staatsblad* (Official Journal) in which it is inserted.

7.5.3 REGULATION ON OCCUPATIONS FOR WHICH A PERSON'S SEX MAY CONSTITUTE A DETERMINING FACTOR (REGULATION PURSUANT TO ARTICLE 5(3), EQUAL TREATMENT ACT)

Article 1

Only occupations which belong to or provide training for one or more of the following categories are considered to be ones for which, because of their nature or the conditions under which they are exercised, sex is a determining factor:

(a) occupations which for physical reasons can only be exercised by persons of a particular sex;

(b) occupations of male or female models who show certain garments by wearing them;

(c) occupations of models for artists, photographers, film-makers, hairdressers, make-up experts and beauty specialists;

(d) occupations within private households which involve personal service, care, nursing or bringing up of or help for one or more persons;

(e) occupations which involve personal care, nursing or help to persons, if the proper performance of the job within the whole of the organization makes it necessary that it is performed by a person of a particular sex;

(f) occupations which involve the attendance or treatment of persons, if because of a serious risk of embarrassment to these persons the proper performance of the job within the whole of the organization makes it necessary that it is performed by a person of a particular sex;

(g) occupations the practice or performance of which is prohibited by law for persons of a particular sex so as to further the protection at work of persons of that sex;

(h) occupations which are practised;

- in other Member States of the European Communities, if in the Member State concerned the occupations are reserved for persons of a particular sex, pursuant to the Directive of the Council of the European Communities of 9 February 1976 (76/207/EEC);

- in countries which are not Member States of the European Communities, if the applicable law reserves these occupations for persons of a particular sex;

(i) occupations in the Armed Forces, to be designated by the Minister for Defence.

Article 2

This Regulation becomes operative on the same day as the Act to amend the legislation on equal treatment of men and women.

Article 3

This Regulation may be cited as the Regulation on occupations for which a person's sex may constitute a determining factor.

8. CASES[1]

8.1   DECISIONS ON EQUALITY IN GENERAL

8.1.1   HIGHER COURTS

Hoge Raad (Supreme Court)
1 October 1980[2]

The *Kieswet* (Election Act) requires married women to be registered under the name of their husband and does not allow them to be registered under their own name. The *Hoge Raad* considered the fact that a very large majority of Dutch women use their husbands' name as a sufficient justification for this provision.

President, Judicial Division of the Raad van State (Council of State)
10 May 1979[3]

HOUSING PERMIT, VALKENBURG.

Article 6(1) of the Housing Regulation 1978 Valkenburg, which excluded women from registration as house-buyers in cases where men could be registered, is in conflict with art. 11(1) first sentence of the International Covenant on Economic, Social and Cultural Rights (New York, 16 December 1966) and with art. 26 of the International Covenant on Civil and Political Rights (New York, 16 December 1966); these Covenants came into effect in the Kingdom of the Netherlands on 11 March 1979.

The decision of the mayor and aldermen, based on the said art. 6(1), can for that reason not be maintained.

---

1   The cases are divided into four sections: §8.1 Equality in general, §8.2 Equal pay, §8.3 Equal treatment, §8.4 Equality in social security. The distinction between equal pay and equal treatment in the Netherlands became less important from the date (1 July 1989) on which equal pay and equal treatment were incorporated in one Act. For uniformity with monographs from other countries, however, the distinction between equal pay and equal treatment is maintained in this chapter. Where there has been an appeal, the case will be listed under the date of the final judgment. Summary proceedings are ranged under 'lower tribunals'. Wherever possible, the names of the parties involved have been mentioned. Many judgments have not been reported in the law journals: NJ, AB or RSV. Where possible, other sources or list numbers are recorded.

2   NJ 1981, 308, and AB 1981, 63.

3   AB 1979, 472.

Hoge Raad
10 December 1982[1]
Binderen/Kaya

RACIAL DISCRIMINATION: PROOF OF DISCRIMINATION.

The housing association, Binderen, did not allot a house to Kaya, a Turk. Was this racial discrimination?

The *Hoge Raad* decided that there was no rule of law which precluded the consideration by the judge of numerical, statistical differences as sufficient basis for the finding that there had been discrimination. Nor was there a rule of law which prevented a conclusion being drawn from these differences indicating *prima facie* evidence of discrimination, and on the basis of this evidence imposed on the party charged with discrimination the onus of proof to show that the refusal was based on admissible reasons.

Hoge Raad
23 December 1983[2]

EQUAL APPLICATION OF THE FREEDOM OF SETTLEMENT RULE.

Article 10 of Regulation 1612/68/EEC grants freedom of settlement to the relations of workers moving within the Community who are citizens of a Member State. A Chinese woman who wanted to stay with her son who lived in the Netherlands and was of Dutch nationality argued that the equality principle implied that the freedom of settlement under art. 10 should apply to her.

The *Hoge Raad* stated that this argument was not valid. It held that the provisions of the Regulation, implementing the rules of the EEC Treaty concerning the free movement of workers within the Community, were intended to further free movement and abolish impediments on the mobility of workers. The principle of equality did not lead to the granting of rights and advantages to relations of persons who do not have the right to free movement of workers equal to those awarded to relations of workers who do have the right to free movement of workers.

---

[1]   NJ 1983, 687 mn EEA.
[2]   NJ 1985, 171 mn EEA.

Hoge Raad
12 October 1984[1]

JUDGE AND LEGISLATURE: ARTICLE 8 OF THE *WET OP HET NEDERLANDERSCHAP* AND ARTICLE 26 OF THE INTERNATIONAL COVENANT ON CIVIL AND POLITICAL RIGHTS.

Article 8 of the *Wet op het Nederlanderschap* (Act on Netherlands Nationality) formerly provided that when a foreign woman married a Dutch citizen, she could obtain Dutch nationality by declaring her wish to do so to the authorities. A similar right was not given to a non-Dutch man who married a Dutch woman.

A man complained that art. 26 of the International Covenant on Civil and Political Rights did not allow this restriction of the right in relation to a woman of foreign nationality.

The *Hoge Raad* considered that various reasonable methods to remove the existing inequality existed. The choice between those methods did not belong to the competence of the courts, but had to be made by the legislature.[2]

Hoge Raad
22 January 1988[3]

ADMITTANCE TO MAIMONIDES LYCEUM.

The plaintiff claimed the right of admittance for his son to the Maimonides Lyceum (school) in Amsterdam. Admittance was refused on the ground that the admissions policy and the constitutional aim on which that policy was founded was to maintain schools for Jewish children in accordance with the *Hallacha*.

The Hoge Raad held that the refusal to admit the plaintiff's son as a student was not unlawful. The admissions policy was endorsed by the interpretation of the admissions rules, laid down in the Constitution. Furthermore, the admissions rules were of a religious nature and aimed at preserving the (religious) Jewish identity of the school. The 'freedom of persuasion' guaranteed to private schools in art. 23 of the Constitution has so much weight that an institution of private education was in principle free to

---

1 AB 1985, 319, *NJCM-Bulletin* 1985, p. 32.
2 New legislation removing this inequality came into force on 1 January 1985. The *Hoge Raad* left unanswered the question whether the prohibition of discrimination had been contravened.
3 NJ 1988, 891.

refuse to admit a child who did not fall within the religious criteria of the admissions rules.

Raad van State, afd. Rechtspraak
5 November 1987[1]
Stokmans/Tilburg Municipality

A licence is required to set up practice as a general practitioner, under art. 5 of the Licensing Order for General Practitioners. The licence is issued by the Municipality.

The plaintiff, a general practitioner seeking a licence to set up practice, was rejected in favour of a female general practitioner, who was furthermore a member of an ethnic minority, in spite of the fact that the plaintiff was recommended by the Proposing Committee.

The *Raad van State* had to consider whether giving immediate effect to the Municipality's decision would be disproportionately damaging to the plaintiff.

The plaintiff claimed:
(a) that the Municipality used the criterion that, in case of sufficient qualification, a woman was to be preferred, whereas it was stated in the advertisement that a woman was to be preferred in case of equal qualifications;
(b) that in the decision the so-called target group policy, which was aimed at ethnic minorities, played an important role although the Municipality had scarcely elaborated that policy and, furthermore, had mentioned that policy in the advertisement only in passing;
(c) that the almost unanimous recommendation of the Proposing Committee, which recommended the plaintiff as the only candidate for the vacancy under consideration, had not, or virtually not, been taken into consideration.

The Municipality stated that the Committee's advice was unacceptable because it had not sufficiently taken into account the principle that, given sufficient qualifications, a woman was to be preferred.

The Municipality declared that Ms A was sufficiently qualified, or at least had qualifications equal to those of the plaintiff, together with the fact that she was of Surinam descent and that in the districts concerned a considerable number of the population came from ethnic minorities.

---

[1]   No R03.87.5728/S6399 71-70.

The President of the *Raad van State* considered that it was sufficiently clear from the advertisement that a clear affinity with ethnic minorities was desirable for the vacancy:

> We are of the opinion that Ms A was equally qualified for the vacancy and was to be preferred. We deem it especially important, in this context, that initially Ms A was recommended by the Committee, and this decision was changed only after the local General Practitioners were consulted. For this latter position, few arguments were put forward.

> We think that the detriment to the plaintiff is not disproportionate to the interests involved in the taking of the decision.

Raad van State
17 March 1988[1]
Baartman/Leiden Municipality

Under art. 5 of the Licensing Order for General Practitioners a licence is required to set up practice as a general practitioner. The licence is issued by the Municipality.

The plaintiff, a general practitioner seeking a licence to set up practice, was rejected in favour of a female general practitioner, in spite of the fact that the plaintiff was recommended by the Proposing Committee.

The *Raad van State* had to consider whether giving immediate effect to the Municipality's decision would be disproportionately damaging to the plaintiff.

The plaintiff stated that, in reaching a decision, the Municipality was not free to apply criteria other than accepting the names in the order they were proposed by the Committee in reaching a decision. Therefore the Municipality should, in his opinion, have issued the licence to him, as he was put first in the recommendation, instead of to Ms A, who was recommended in the second place.

The President considered that the argument that no criteria other than the order of names were admissible was unfounded.

He further stated that the policy operated by the Municipality to let 30 per cent of the total number of general practitioner positions be filled by women was made clear in the advertisement. Furthermore, such a policy, that sufficiently qualified women were to be preferred, could not be considered unacceptable. Since both candidates were qualified for the vacancy, the policy referred to was sufficient justification for a deviation from the Committee's recommendation.

---

[1]   No R03.88.0491/S5136 99-92.

The damage to the plaintiff was not disproportionate to the interests involved in giving effect to the decision.

Centrale Raad van Beroep
16 February 1989[1]

The plaintiffs appealed against the deduction of 1.85 per cent from their wages for January and February 1983 on the basis of the Act on Temporary Deduction from Salaries in Education and Science (WIISO: *Wet Interim Inhouding Salarissen Onderwijs*).[2] They referred to the right, under art. 7 of the International Covenant on Economic, Social and Cultural Rights (New York, December 1966) to equal remuneration for work of equal value without distinction of any kind.

The *Rechtbank* ruled that the provision referred to had direct effect, and could be relied upon by a citizen in a situation where equality of pay based on equal value was prejudiced. That applied in this case.

The *Centrale Raad van Beroep*, however, stated that the provisions of the Covenant could only have direct effect when they were sufficiently clear and to the point and the situation in which application of the provisions was requested was sufficiently structured and concrete. Moreover, direct effect of a provision was only to be presumed in identical or nearly identical cases, and not when the work was (only) of equal value. The *Raad* considered it very significant that the functions with which the plaintiffs compared their work were not carried out under the same authority.

These considerations led the *Centrale Raad* to the conclusion that art. 7 did not have direct effect in the plaintiffs' case. The plaintiffs, therefore, could not rely on the provision.

8.1.2   COURTS OF APPEAL

There are no relevant judgments of courts of appeal under this heading.

---

1   NJ/AB 1989, 164; TAR 1989, p. 77.
2   Act of 12 January 1983, Stb 1983, 1.

8.2 DECISIONS ON EQUALITY IN PAY[1]

8.2.1 HIGHER COURTS

Hoge Raad
13 November 1987[2]
Gielen/St. Bavo

EQUAL PAY. STATUS OF EQUAL TREATMENT COMMITTEE.

A housekeeping assistant (female) earned less than a cleaning employee (male). The woman filed a claim for equal pay. The difference in pay had an 'historical background': under influence of the situation in the labour market in the past the employees concerned were recruited on different pay levels.

The Equal Treatment Committee felt that it concerned work of (nearly) equal value. This implied an obligation to pay equal remuneration.

The *Kantonrechter* (Cantonal Judge) considered that the jobs clearly differed. Because of the differences, the men were attracted by one job, and the women by the other, apart from the remuneration. Both men and women worked as housekeeping assistants. The remuneration was not discriminatory. It would be an improper use of the Equal Pay Act, therefore, if the claim were awarded. The claim was rejected.

In a new Opinion the Committee repeated that on the basis of job evaluation the work was of (nearly) equal value and that the woman was entitled to equal pay. According to the Committee, this claim was not invalidated merely because the difference in remuneration was not caused by a difference in sex.

On appeal, the *Rechtbank* set aside the judgment of the *Kantonrechter* and asked for a further Opinion.

The Committee gave the same Opinion (for the third time).

Four more housekeeping assistants, employed by the same employer, who sought the Committee's advice received the same Opinion.

The *Rechtbank* allowed the claim. The employer appealed to the *Hoge Raad*.

---

[1] Extensive use is made in this section, and in the section on equal treatment, of A.-M. GERRITSEN, *Rechtspraak gelijke behandeling m/v*, Leiden, 1987.

[2] NJ 1989, 698.

The *Hoge Raad* held:

(1) The view that, when an employer is bound by a collective agreement, the employees cannot file a claim pursuant to art. 2 of the Equal Pay Act even when their jobs were not mentioned in the collective agreement concerned was not correct. This view would prejudice the protection intended under the Equal Pay Act and could not be deemed to be right for that reason, as it was not supported either by the wording or the history of the Act.

(2) Since the woman received less pay than the man she compared herself with, it was irrelevant that the difference in pay was due to historical reasons. It was also irrelevant that both jobs were open to men and women, whereas within the jobs women and men were paid equally.

(3) Considering the specific expertise of the Committee and the importance which was, in view of art. 16 of the Equal Pay Act, to be attached to its Opinions, sound reasoning was necessary to reach a decision at variance from such an Opinion. It was for the employer to present such reasoning when he had been declared to be in the wrong by the Committee.

Hoge Raad
24 April 1992[1]
Bouma/KLM

Bouma was employed by KLM from 1973 as a crew member. On 1 December 1985 she became purser. On 1 January 1977 the terms of employment of the employer had been equalized and a new regulation for crew members was introduced. There remained a separate scale for male pursers who were at that moment in service (key corps) who therefore kept their higher salary. In this procedure Bouma claimed a declaration that KLM had violated the Equal Pay Act and the Equal Treatment Act, plus back pay from 1 December 1985 on, supposing that her salary was to be calculated in conformity with scale 2a. The Cantonal Judge turned these claims down. The District Court confirmed the judgment of the Cantonal Judge. The *Hoge Raad* considered that Bouma's claims had to be judged, in so far as they were pertinent to the period until 1 July 1989, in conformity with the Equal Pay Act, and from that time on in conformity with the Equal Treatment Act, in connection with article 1637ij of the Civil Code. The Equal Treatment Act had, in so far as wages are concerned, the same intention as the Equal Pay Act. Direct discrimination in the field of pay was forbidden, unless there was an exception covered by the Act, and indirect discrimination was forbidden if no objective justification could be shown.

There was, at most, indirect discrimination in this case. Bouma received for work of equal value less pay than the pursers belonging to the key corps.

---

[1]   JAR 1992, 14.

The decisive questions were whether there had been indirect discrimination and if so, whether KLM had shown that there was an objective justification for that discrimination. The first question had to be answered affirmatively, the second negatively. The pay Bouma received was not up to the standards of the Equal Pay Act and/or the Equal Treatment Act.

Centrale Raad van Beroep
29 December 1987[1]
Lodel /Algemeen Directeur van het Medisch Centrum Alkmaar

EQUAL PAY. PROMOTION.

The plaintiff worked as head of the operating room, location North, of the *Medisch Centrum Alkmaar* (MCA), with the rank of ward matron. Head of the operating room of the MCA location South was her male colleague, J. van den Berg. This colleague was promoted to the rank of ward-master A with effect from 1 January 1979, a fact which became known to the plaintiff in October 1982. The plaintiff then requested promotion, which was refused.

The plaintiff filed a complaint with the Equal Treatment Committee. The Equal Treatment Committee decided on 16 April 1984 that the MCA had acted in contravention of art. 1(1) of the Equal Treatment Act (Civil Servants), as there was a difference between the wages of the plaintiff and the male colleague with whom she was comparing herself.

The defendants sought to justify their decision.

The *Centrale Raad van Beroep* considered whether the defendants, weighing all interests, could have properly reached the decision or whether the decision otherwise contravened any principle of law or any general principle of administration.

The *Centrale Raad* held that the decision could pass that test. The immediate cause for the man's promotion was that he had qualities (beyond those of the plaintiff) which caused him to be involved in the preparation of the integration within the hospital, bearing in mind that he would be head of the integrated ward.

Moreover, the pay which the plaintiff received was (and the plaintiff did not contest that) adequate in itself.

The *Centrale Raad* held that the defendants had reached the decision by acceptable means.

---

[1]   AB 1986/222, unreported.

8.2.2   COURTS OF APPEAL

Rechtbank Amsterdam
26 March 1980 and 11 March 1981[1]
Prenatal

EQUAL PAY. TASK OF THE COMMITTEE.

The pay of a (female) registration clerk was lower than that of a (male) 'receiver of incoming goods'. The fact that her male colleague loaded and unloaded trucks was in the view of the plaintiff no reason for the difference in pay. She claimed payment of back pay.

It became clear, *inter alia* through a *Loontechnische Dienst* (Service on technical matters concerning wages) investigation, that the jobs of 'registration clerk' and 'receiver of incoming goods' were not of nearly equal value. But the jobs of 'registration clerk' and 'filler' were of nearly equal value. In this case, where the plaintiff's claim was founded on a comparison of her job with the job of a 'receiver of incoming goods', the Equal Treatment Committee could only issue an opinion founded on that comparison. There was no question of unequal pay.

The *Rechtbank* considered that the Committee or the *Kantonrechter* (first instance) should have made a closer examination of the equality in value of the plaintiff's job and that of a 'filler', the more so as, generally speaking, it could not be expected that a person who asked the Committee for advice had sufficient expertise in the evaluation of the jobs to be compared. The Court asked the Committee for a further Opinion.

In its judgment of 11 March 1981 the *Rechtbank* annulled the judgment of the *Kantonrechter*, who had dismissed the claim because, as stated in the Committee's first Opinion, there was no question of work of nearly equal value. The Court ordered the employer to pay back pay.

Rechtbank 's-Hertogenbosch
2 March 1984 and 2 May 1985[2]
Panhuyzen-De Bruijn/St. Lambertus

EQUAL PAY, STATUS OF COMMITTEE OPINION. MEANING OF THE TERM 'USUALLY RECEIVES'.

Fourteen female employees of a hospital filed a complaint with the Equal Treatment Committee. Household department assistants, a kitchen assistant and a laundry assistant (all female) all compared their jobs with that

---

1   GERRITSEN I, p. 2.
2   Rolno 3387/82, 3388/82 and 3389/82.

of a (male) household assistant; a female receptionist and a female coffee counter attendant compared themselves with a male colleague who held the same job. Most women chose a second person to compare themselves with (a cleaning assistant, laundry assistant or coffee counter attendant). All of the women earned less than these men.

The Committee's view was that the work of each female employee was of (nearly) equal value to the work of at least one male worker they compared themselves with in each case. Each woman was entitled to pay equal to that of the man. Three of the women filed a claim for equal pay.

The *Rechtbank* held that the wages for performing a job which had been held by one worker only (and then only on a temporary basis) was not the pay the worker usually received (art. 2 of the Equal Pay Act). The employers' plea that the women could not in good faith refer to the Committee's Opinion because this Opinion was effected incorrectly was dismissed by the Court. The judge was free to interpret the Opinion. The judge could not ask the Committee to conduct a further investigation. The work of a household department assistant was not of (nearly) equal value to the work of a male household assistant and that of various other male colleagues. The claim was dismissed.

Rechtbank Utrecht
12 June 1985 and 2 July 1986[1]
Bruinsma/Pegus

EQUAL PAY. STATUS OF COMMITTEE'S OPINION.

The plaintiff and the man she compared herself with were both employed as clerical assistants in the salary administration department, she as an assistant clerk, he as a 'clerk A'. There was a difference in rank of 15 points between the jobs. The woman considered that the difference in pay was a consequence of the job ranking and contrary to the Equal Pay Act and claimed back pay.

The Equal Treatment Committee stated that although the difference in job ranking was not large, there was no question of work of nearly equal value. An attempt by the Committee to find another man with whom to compare the plaintiff failed. After the Committee had explained how, notwithstanding the fact that the difference of rank was not large, it nevertheless believed that the work was not of nearly equal value, the *Kantonrechter* followed the Committee's Opinion and dismissed the claim.

---

1   No 624/84 HB, unreported.

The *Rechtbank* rejected the plaintiff's criticism of the job ranking system. An investigation by another body also resulted in a small difference in ranking, which could result in classifying the jobs in different scales. The judge was not bound to follow the Committee's view, but could depart from it on good grounds. In this case, however, there were no such grounds. The claim was dismissed.

8.2.3   LOWER TRIBUNALS

Kantonrechter Eindhoven
11 May 1978[1]

JUSTIFICATION FOR UNEQUAL PAY WHEN JOBS ARE OF NEARLY EQUAL VALUE.

A medical representative, who had been in employment since 1965, found out that she received less pay than her male colleague. The latter had recently been promoted to sales-supervisor. The woman's new male colleague also received more pay than she did. She took the view that she was receiving unequal pay. According to the Equal Treatment Committee, the jobs of medical representative and sales-supervisor were not of equal value. The Committee made, of its own accord, a comparison with the new colleague. The latter held the same job as the woman but received more pay because of his education, age and experience. There was, in the Committee's view, no question of unequal pay.

In the proceedings before the *Kantonrechter* the employer claimed a termination of the contract of employment. The judge made an award accordingly.

Central Committee for Clerical Personnel in Newspaper Companies
30 July 1979[2]

BOMILO (PAYMENT SYSTEMS IN COLLECTIVE AGREEMENTS).

In the applicable collective agreement minimum wages for different jobs had been set out. Moreover, the maximum scope was indicated within which the employer could pay individual employees more than the minimum pay provided by the collective agreement. This system is called *'Bomilo'*. Through use of the *Bomilo* system a male canvasser was paid more than a female canvasser. The woman considered that this difference in pay was not justified.

---

[1]   GERRITSEN I, p. 1.
[2]   GERRITSEN I, p. 4.

The Equal Treatment Committee stated that the employer had a discretion when using the *Bomilo* technique. In exercising this discretion, however, the employer could not contravene the Equal Pay Act. In this case there was unequal pay.

The same Opinion was given to a colleague of the first plaintiff.

The Central Committee stated that the Equal Treatment Committee's Opinion was ill-founded. The man's higher pay was based on experience and professional skill. The woman could not prove there had been discrimination. The claim was dismissed.

8.3   DECISIONS ON EQUAL TREATMENT

8.3.1   HIGHER COURTS

Hoge Raad
21 November 1986[1]
Beets-Proper/van Lanschot

RETIREMENT AGE.

According to the applicable pension scheme the date of retirement was the first day of the month following the month within which the male participant attained 65 years of age, and the female participant 60 years of age. The plaintiff, a woman, became 60 years old in August 1982.

In the view of the Equal Treatment Committee this provision in the pension scheme did not do justice to women who did not need the benefit of an earlier retirement age. The right to choose between using the so-called *vut*-measure (early retirement measure) and continuing to work until the age of 65 was denied to women by the imposition of the protective measure. This was direct discrimination. The Committee stated that this view necessarily implied that the provision for the termination of contracts of employment of women of 60 years would have to be abandoned.

In summary proceedings, a woman claimed continuance in her job and payment of wages up to the moment the contract of employment could be lawfully terminated.

The *Rechtbank* (District Court) ruled that the exception in art. 1637ij(1) of the Civil Code for 'benefits or claims under any pension scheme' was intended to leave the whole issue of pensions, including the matter of retirement ages, unchanged until it was regulated in a separate Act. The provision in the pension scheme that led to the termination of the contract of employment between the parties concerned was not null and void. The claim was rejected.

On appeal, the *Hof* (Court) ruled that there was a close connection between the termination of a contract of employment and the commencement of a pension. This was also evident from the fact that female employees built up a pension with 2 per cent of the annual basic pay, and male employees with only 1.75 per cent a year. For women there was also a special opportunity to work short time. The exception in art. 1637ij of the Civil Code ('the expression "conditions of employment" does not include benefits or claims under any pension scheme') was applicable. The decision was confirmed.

---

[1]   NJ 1987, 351.

The *Hoge Raad* referred the case to the ECJ for a preliminary ruling. The question put was whether Directive 76/207/EEC allowed Member States the freedom not to include among the conditions of employment, in respect of which equal treatment for men and women must be laid down pursuant to the Directive, an express or implied condition concerning the termination of the contract of employment on the ground of the age attained by the employee, where that condition relates to the age at which the employee becomes entitled to a pension.

The ECJ stated that the word 'dismissal' in art. 5(1) of the Directive must be given a wide meaning. An age limit for the compulsory dismissal of workers pursuant to an employer's general policy concerning retirement fell within the term 'dismissal' construed in that manner, even if the dismissal involved the grant of a retirement pension.[1]

The Court also stated that art. 1(2) of the Directive, which excludes social security matters from the scope of the Directive, had to be interpreted strictly. In consequence, the exception to the prohibition of discrimination on grounds of sex contained in art. 7(1)(a) of Directive 79/7/EEC applied only to the determination of retirement age for the purposes of granting old-age and retirement pensions and to the consequences thereof for other social security benefits.

Article 5(1) of Directive 76/207/EEC had to be interpreted as meaning that it did not allow Member States the freedom to exempt from the application of the principle of equality of treatment an express or implied condition in a contract of employment concluded on the basis of a collective agreement, if that condition had the effect of terminating the contract of employment on the ground of the age attained by the employee, and the relevant age was determined by the age (different for men and women) at which the employee became entitled to a retirement pension.

The *Hoge Raad* stated that the *Rechtbank* had incorrectly interpreted the law. The condition that the contract of employment was terminated when the female employee reached the age of 60 was null and void. In law the contract of employment terminated when the age of 65 had been reached.

---

[1]   *Beets-Proper* v. *van Lanschot Bankiers*, Case 262/84, [1986] ECR 773 (ECJ).

Hoge Raad
24 June 1988[1]
Dekker/VJV

UNLAWFUL ACT. REFUSAL TO ENTER INTO A CONTRACT OF EMPLOYMENT
BECAUSE OF THE PREGNANCY OF THE CANDIDATE. RISK THAT
MATERNITY PAY MAY BE REFUSED.

Dekker had applied for a job in an educational centre for young adults.
She told the recruitment committee on 15 June 1981 that she was three
months pregnant. After being proposed by the recruitment committee as the
most suitable candidate for the job, Dekker received by letter of 10 July 1981
notification that she would not be appointed.

The employer had reached this decision on the following grounds. By
virtue of the applicable regulations the *Risicofonds* (the body which
administered sickness and maternity benefits) was entitled to refuse
maternity benefits to Dekker because she would have been pregnant when
her duties would have commenced on 1 September 1981. On the other hand,
the regulations obliged the employer to pay an employee's full pay during
the first year of incapacity, including pregnancy and maternity. This would
mean that VJV would, for financial reasons, not be able to appoint a
substitute for Dekker while she was absent by reason of her pregnancy and
maternity leave.

If the employer was not able to appoint a substitute for Dekker during
her maternity leave, this might result in a lower subsidy from the Ministry of
Education and Science, and therefore jeopardize the work and employment in
the employer's establishment.

The *Hoge Raad* referred the case to the ECJ for a preliminary ruling on
the following questions:

(1) Is an employer directly or indirectly in breach of the principle of equal
    treatment referred to in articles 2(1) and 3(1) of Directive 76/207/EEC if
    he refuses to enter into a contract of employment with an applicant
    found suitable by him, where such refusal is on the ground of the
    possible adverse consequences for him arising from employing a
    woman who is pregnant at the time of the application, because of a
    Government Regulation concerning incapacity to work which treats
    inability to work because of pregnancy and confinement in the same
    way as inability to work because of illness?
(2) Does it make any difference to the answer to Question 1 that there were
    no male candidates?
(3) Is it compatible with articles 2 and 3:

---

1   NJ 1988, 1002.

(a) that when it is established that the principle of equal treatment has been violated to the detriment of the rejected applicant, in order for a claim based on that violation to be upheld, there is an additional requirement of fault on the part of the employer?

(b) that when such violation of principle is established, the employer, on his part, can still rely on grounds of legal justification, in the absence of any cases referred to in article 2(2) - (4)?

(4) If the requirement of fault as referred to under Question 3 may be imposed, or grounds of legal justification may be invoked, is it sufficient to establish the absence of fault or the presence of grounds of legal justification that the employer incurs the risks as described in the facts, or do articles 2 and 3 have to be interpreted to mean that he should bear those risks, unless he is completely certain that the payment because of incapacity to work will be refused, or that he will suffer a loss of training places and he has done everything possible in order to prevent this occurring?

The ECJ held that an employer who refuses to enter into a contract of employment with a woman who is otherwise thought suitable because of possible adverse consequences arising out of her pregnancy, even if these arise from Government Regulations, acts contrary to arts 2(1) and 3(1) of Directive 76/207/EEC. Such a decision would amount to discrimination even where there was no male candidate for the post in question.[1]

Hoge Raad
25 November 1988[2]
Riete Pot

GRADING OF EMPLOYEES WHEN ENTERING EMPLOYMENT.

Employees were graded according to directives of the Ministry of Education and Science, based on qualifications and recent salary. Previous experience was not taken into account.

The Equal Treatment Committee stated that educational qualifications were in principle an indirectly discriminatory criterion, since more men than women have such qualifications. However, the criterion was reasonably appropriate for grading purposes. The aim of preventing pay reductions justified the non-application of the education-level criterion. There was no indirect discrimination.

The woman stated that the unequal wage was an infringement of the Equal Treatment Act and art. 1637ij of the Civil Code, thus amounting to an

---

[1] *Dekker* v. *Stichting Vormingscentrum voor Jong Volwassenen*, Case 177/88, [1990] ECR I-3941 (ECJ).

[2] NJ 1989, 730.

unlawful act. The damages claimed amounted to the sum which should have been paid (but was not paid) in wages.

The *Kantonrechter* (Cantonal Judge) held that, generally speaking, more women than men were forced to interrupt their careers in order to look after their family. The criterion based on recent pay was therefore especially detrimental to women. If experience was left out of consideration in grading, the application of the criterion of recent pay received could not be justified on the ground of avoiding a reduction in pay, in comparison with pay previously earned. A hypothetical career and knowledge of life were non-objectifiable concepts. Grading on the basis of these concepts might lead to inequalities. Grading on the basis of education and experience made more sense.

The *Rechtbank* (District Court) confirmed this judgment.

The *Hoge Raad* held that the *Rechtbank* and the *Kantonrechter* had correctly and on good grounds decided that the employer had acted contrary to art. 1637ij .

8.3.2   COURTS OF APPEAL

Rechtbank Utrecht
6 February 1985
Heidi Pross/Stimezo[1]

PREGNANCY. NON-EXTENSION OF CONTRACT OF EMPLOYMENT.

The contract of employment of Ms Pross (on a fixed term for six months) was due to be extended by another six months. Because she was pregnant, the extension was limited to one month.

The Equal Treatment Committee stated that referral to pregnancy amounted to direct or (if it was understood as referring to family circumstances) indirect discrimination covered by art. 1637ij(1) of the Civil Code. Ms Pross claimed that the termination of her contract of employment was unlawful and claimed payment of her wages.

The *Kantonrechter* (Cantonal Judge) held that the Equal Treatment Committee's Opinion was irrelevant. Ms Pross feared difficulties for her social security benefits if the contract of employment was terminated by her own initiative, and therefore asked the employer to base his decision to terminate the contract of employment after one month on her pregnancy. There was nothing to indicate that the employee had entered into the contract of employment for one month under pressure. Without that contract of

---

1   GERRITSEN I, p. 243.

employment she ran the risk, as a person dismissed of her own accord, of not qualifying for unemployment benefit. An appeal under the Equal Treatment Act was certainly not appropriate for an employee who, although only in service for a short period, had resolved to get pregnant on short notice and thus, at least for a time, would not be able to work. It was not surprising that the employer found this matter difficult, and that had nothing to do with what the Act intended to combat.

The *Rechtbank* (District Court) held that Ms Pross had to prove that the contract signed by her did not conform to her real wish. She could appeal under the Equal Treatment Act, but had not done so within the time limit of two months after the dismissal or after the termination of the contract of employment. She could not avoid the time limit by seeking a declaration from the judge that the termination was unlawful.

Gerechtshof 's-Hertogenbosch
17 April 1984[1]
Van den Broek and Vereijken/van Dam

DISMISSAL. ONUS OF PROOF.

An undertaking asked, for reasons of re-organization, for permission to dismiss 19 employees, 10 male and nine female. There was to be no woman left in the department. The selection criteria were availability for service, seniority, and possibly diminished availability because of sick leave.

The Equal Treatment Committee stated that the criteria of availability and seniority in themselves did not amount to direct discrimination between men and women, but their application was detrimental to women in the production process. The employer had not shown that the availability criterion had been applied in such a way that, using objective yardsticks, another outcome would have been detrimental to the undertaking. The amount of sick leave could be influenced by relations with superiors and by the atmosphere in the department. Nor had a justification for the application of the seniority rule been put forward. The Committee concluded that there had been indirect discrimination.

The plaintiffs claimed, in summary proceedings, that the re-organization should not be put into effect as long as the selection criteria did not conform to the Equal Treatment Act, and that the requests for dismissal should be suspended.

The President of the *Rechtbank* stated that the Opinion of the Committee could not result in preventing the re-organization from

---

[1]   NJ 1985, 202; *NJCM-Bulletin* 1984, p. 381; National Ombudsman, Report 84.00023, *NJCM-Bulletin* 1987, p. 64.

proceeding. The plaintiffs' interests did not justify the suspension or withdrawal of the reorganization plan. The employer's explanation was justified. The claims were dismissed.

The *Gerechtshof* 's-Hertogenbosch held that the suspension or withdrawal of the re-organization as a whole was not justified. The Equal Treatment Act did not require preferential treatment when women were under-represented. The fact that no provision had been made for any of the women provided *prima facie* evidence of indirect discrimination. The women were not to be dismissed before the Committee had given its view.

The National Ombudsman stated that the Director of the *Gewestelijk Arbeidsbureau* (GAB: the Regional Labour Office, the authority charged with issuing permission for dismissal) should have suspended the permission for dismissal. It was negligent that he did not do so. The failure to suspend might not have been negligent if an investigation had been made, the results of which would not have led to suspension. Moreover, the outcome of the investigation should have served as a basis for that decision.

Rechtbank Rotterdam
27 June 1986[1]
De Jong/Gerretsen and van den Blink

ARTICLE 2 *BUITENGEWOON BESLUIT ARBEIDSVERHOUDINGEN* (BBA)
(LABOUR RELATIONS DECREE 1945). DIRECT EFFECT.

Article 6 of the *Buitengewoon Besluit Arbeidsverhoudingen* (BBA: Labour Relations Decree) stated that an employment relationship should not be terminated by the employer or the employee without the consent of the director of the local labour office (GAB). Article 2(1)(d) of the BBA exempted from the scope of this Decree among others 'female employees who perform only or principally domestic work or personal services in the household of private individuals'.

Ms de Jong, a cleaning woman in a private household, was dismissed without the consent of the director of the local employment office. The question she put to the court was: should art. 2(1)(d) of the BBA be considered ineffective because it was contrary to Directive 76/207/EEC?

The *Rechtbank* considered that it did not rule out the possibility that Ms de Jong could argue that art. 2(1)(d) of the BBA was contrary to the Directive, because the conditions the ECJ put forward for direct effect of Directives appeared to have been fulfilled. This did not mean, however, that Ms de Jong could invoke direct effect in this procedure against Gerretsen and van den Blink. It should be noted that the conflict with the Directive could be

---

[1]   NJ 1988, 32.

removed in different ways, and it was up to the Netherlands legislature to choose between the different possibilities.

Gerechtshof 's-Gravenhage
9 July 1987[1]
De Vries and Ombudsvrouw/The Netherlands
(Minister for Education and Science)

DIFFERENT TREATMENT OF PART-TIME WORKERS.

Teachers who worked less than 32 hours per week (or worked less than 20 hours per week and were 55 years of age or older) were not considered for short time. Short time was cheaper and could create employment. In the teaching profession more women than men worked part-time. The Minister expected that the new employment, on the other hand, would be beneficial to women, and also thought it favourable for women that there would be more part-time jobs.

The Equal Treatment Committee stated that, since it was mainly women who were working part-time in the teaching profession, the Regulation was indirectly discriminatory. The justification submitted did not outweigh the ban on unequal treatment of men and women.

The Minister disregarded the Committee's view.

The President of the *Rechtbank* (District Court) ruled that it was to be expected that the extra hours which would become available as a consequence of this regulation would be taken up by part-time workers, therefore particularly by women. The apparent indirect discrimination was however justified. Claims to suspend the regulation and claims for damages were dismissed.

The *Gerechtshof* (Regional Court) considered that the total package of measures indicated that it did not involve serious detriment to women. The disqualification for short-time work did not prejudice women. From figures, subsequently available, it was however apparent that the measure in fact had a favourable effect on women's employment. The Court found that the conflicting effects balanced one another. There was no unlawful act.

---

[1]   NJ 1989, 21.

Rechtbank Amsterdam
18 November 1987[1]
Hallen/van Kollen

ONUS OF PROOF. STATUS OF COMMITTEE'S OPINION.

A man applied for the job of receptionist. One of the employer's staff made it clear that the man was the only candidate for the job and that he was eligible. The member of staff informed the man, however, that the managers who had to approve the appointment preferred a female receptionist.

The Equal Treatment Committee stated that there had been unequal treatment in the offer of the job and the procedure followed for filling the vacancy.

The *Kantonrechter* (Cantonal Judge) considered that the prohibition of discrimination in offering a job and the procedure followed for filling a vacancy was to be regarded as a measure directed at the employer which, when infringed, resulted in an unlawful act. The judge allowed the man to present evidence showing whether in fact there had been discrimination. Subsequently he decided that sufficient evidence had not been furnished.

The *Rechtbank* (District Court) considered that the Committee's view did not have the force of an Opinion binding on parties. The reasoning of the Committee's view was not such that it should lead to a reversal of the burden of proof, and the *Kantonrechter* correctly allowed the man to produce evidence to support his claim.

The *Rechtbank* rejected the claim that the *Kantonrechter* had violated his duty to give reasons by not stating why he had departed from the Committee's view.

Rechtbank Arnhem
24 December 1987[2]
Severijnen/Roelantstichting

PREGNANCY. ENTERING INTO A CONTRACT OF EMPLOYMENT.

A speech therapist revealed on her first working day (during the probation period) that she was pregnant. Shortly afterwards she received a written contract of employment and, at the same time, notice of her dismissal. The employer's school, where the plaintiff worked, specialized in the education of children with 'minimal brain damage'. For that reason the

---

[1]   NJ 1988, 695.
[2]   NJ 1988, 309; Prg 1988, No 2888.

employer was opposed to a temporary replacement and therefore to the plaintiff's foreseeable absence.

The Equal Treatment Committee stated that a dismissal during the probationary period could not evade the rules which were so fundamental that their circumvention would be an affront to the rule of law. Article 1637ij of the Civil Code was such a rule. The prohibition of discrimination in making an appointment and the procedures to fill a vacancy would be meaningless if the effects of the prohibition could be nullified. At the time of the application for the job the plaintiff was not yet pregnant. She had been dismissed because of her pregnancy. This was direct discrimination between men and women.

The woman claimed that the dismissal was null and void and in violation of art. 1637ij of the Civil Code and claimed payment of wages and damages.

The *Kantonrechter* (Cantonal Judge) held that the termination of a contract of employment during the probationary period was prohibited if the termination constituted discrimination between men and women. There was discrimination if there was a direct connection between the termination and the employee's pregnancy, as only women could get pregnant. In this case there was such a direct connection. The termination was valid but the employer had to pay damages. The employer had violated his duties as a *bona fide* employer. The employer was ordered to supplement the unemployment benefit and to provide compensation fixed at Hfl 13,000, roughly a year's pay.

The *Rechtbank* (District Court) held that the *Kantonrechter* had properly considered that art. 1637ij of the Civil Code prohibited the making of a distinction between men and women when terminating a contract of employment, and that this also covered a termination during a probationary period. The prohibition of discrimination when dismissing staff applied to this case.

The foreseeable absence was, in the Court's view, the inevitable and direct consequence of the pregnancy, to such an extent that in fact a direct relation between that pregnancy and the termination of the employment contract had to be assumed.

The complaint that the *Kantonrechter* had, in applying art. 1637ij of the Civil Code, unfairly neglected to weigh the parties' interests against each other did not succeed. The issue whether there was a question of discrimination could only be judged by considering the employer's conduct in the particular case. The underlying interests of employer and employee were, as regards that issue, in principle of no consequence. Such a weighing of interests, moreover, could lead to the prohibition of discrimination in certain circumstances becoming illusory and that could, considering the sanctions under the Regulation, not have been the legislature's intention.

The Court ruled that the damages awarded were appropriate.

Gerechtshof 's-Gravenhage
17 February 1988[1]
HOS-Nota

INDIRECT DISCRIMINATION. REFERENCE GROUP.

According to the *Herstructurering Onderwijs Salariëring* system (HOS: restructuring of wages in education and teaching) the grading in the new type of primary schools corresponded to pay previously received. Former heads of infant schools, mainly women, were thus on a lower grade than former heads of primary schools of the old type.

The Equal Treatment Committee stated that this criterion amounted to *prima facie* evidence of indirect discrimination. The previous level of wages was not relevant to the job. This was not a justified distinction. The fact that another aspect of the grading was mainly favourable to women was no objective justification, nor were the financial and employment motives. There was thus indirect discrimination.

The President of the *Rechtbank* (District Court) ruled that it was not mainly women who were directly disadvantaged by the HOS-system. Of those who were disadvantaged, 43 per cent were female and 57 per cent male. It was not right to choose from those covered by the measure a relatively small group and compare them with another (also relatively small) group. The claim was dismissed.

The *Gerechtshof* (Regional Court) held that the plaintiffs had not convincingly countered the State's defence concerning the weight of the management experience of the former heads of infants schools, in relation to the comparable experience of former heads of primary schools of the old type. The State's defence on this point could serve as an objective justification. There was no infringement of the Equal Treatment Act.

---

[1]   NJ 1988, 919.

8.3.3 LOWER TRIBUNALS

Rechtbank 's-Gravenhage
22 June 1981
Gerechtshof 's-Gravenhage
13 May 1982[1]

The *Besluit Benoemingseisen Politieambtenaren* (Decree concerning qualifications for appointment as police officers) provided that men had to have a minimum height of 1.70 m. The minimum height required for women was 1.65 m.; this requirement had not been formally laid down. The Department of Justice gave as reason for these requirements that in this way it was possible to standardize equipment and clothes, and that a minimum height could be of some importance in exercising the function of police officer.

The Equal Treatment Committee (civil servants) stated that the text of the Decree conflicted with art. 1(1) of the Equal Treatment Act (Civil Servants).[2] Different height requirements were only allowed if these requirements were functional; if a requirement in practice had an adverse effect on persons of one sex, different requirements could be applied to remove that inequality. *In casu* the requirements were not functional: standardization was also possible based on another height, and a minimum height did not appear to be necessary to exercise the profession of police officer satisfactorily. There was thus an incompatibility with the Equal Treatment Act.

Ambtenarengerecht 's-Hertogenbosch
9 May 1983[3]

The plaintiff, recommended for appointment, was not appointed because she was married and her husband had disposable earnings.

The Equal Treatment Committee (civil servants) stated that the right to work was an individual right which could not be made dependent on the occupation of a partner. If in appointments the economic position of members of the plaintiff's family were taken into account, in the majority of cases women would in practice be disadvantaged in obtaining work. There was indirect discrimination, contrary to art. 1(5) of the Equal Treatment Act.[4]

The woman appealed to the *Ambtenarengerecht* (Civil Servants' Tribunal).

---

[1] NJ 1983, 190.
[2] Since 1 July 1989, art. l(a) of the Equal Treatment Act.
[3] Rolno 82/110.
[4] As it then was: now art. 1(a) of the Equal Treatment Act.

The President of the *Ambtenarengerecht* considered that the Municipal Board (which had the authority to appoint) could not in good faith deviate from the proposal to appoint the plaintiff. The Municipal Board was not expert and did not have other expert data at its disposal. The interests of teaching should be put first and foremost in any decision concerning the appointment of a teacher. The woman should be allowed to work as a teacher until a decision was reached at the final proceedings.

The *Ambtenarengerecht* held that a preference for the plaintiff was clear from the school head's proposal, based on educational grounds. Within reason, the Board had no cause to deviate from this proposal on educational grounds. If the Municipal Board wanted to do so, their line of thought should have been the same for everybody. This was in conflict with the notion of careful preparation of decisions. The earnings position of the candidates had not been examined. There was a defect in the decision-making. The provisions of the Equal Treatment Act should have been borne in mind when the decision was reached. It was not evident that there were interests at stake in this case of equal importance to those protected by the Equal Treatment Act. The decision was annulled.

Rechtbank 's-Gravenhage
25 September 1984[1]

For a temporary job under measure *Werkgelegenheidsprojecten Onderwijs* (employment in teaching projects) the only unemployed persons who could be considered were those who could claim unemployment benefits chargeable to the Department, or benefits covered by the WWV (Act on Unemployment Benefits) or the RWW (Unemployed Social Assistance Regulations). A married woman was not entitled to unemployment benefits under the WWV unless she was considered to be the breadwinner or was separated from her husband. When entitlement to a benefit was covered by the RWW the earnings of a spouse or partner were taken into account.

The Equal Treatment Committee (civil servants) held that the question whether or not a person is married, and the earnings of the partner, could not be a factor in recruitment and selection. The application of the breadwinner criterion placed the majority of women at a disadvantage. In this case there had been direct and/or indirect discrimination.

The President of the *Rechtbank* held that the measure could not be put into effect as long as the jobs covered by the measure could not be given to married women who did not qualify for a WWV or RWW benefit.

---

1   GERRITSEN I, p. 559.

Kantonrechter Rotterdam
6 and 27 September 1984[1]
Pet/Crédit Lyonnais

There was a provision in a pension scheme that the retirement date for women was the first day of the month following the 60th birthday and for men the first day of the month following the 65th birthday. The plaintiff attained her pension date on 1 November 1982. The contract of employment was then extended. According to the plaintiff this extension was for an unspecified period, according to the employer until 1 January 1983.

The Equal Treatment Committee held that the pension scheme did not do justice to women who were not in need of the protective measure. Women were deprived of the option of choosing to use the so-called 'voluntary retirement measure' or to continue working until the age of 65. There was thus direct discrimination. This view did not mean, however, that the women's contracts of employment terminated at the age of 60.

The plaintiff claimed payment of wages and a declaration that the contract of employment continued. In summary proceedings it was held that the employer had to allow her to continue to work.

Permission for dismissal, requested by the employer, was refused by the director of the GAB (regional labour office).

The *Kantonrechter* (Cantonal Judge) held that the contract of employment had continued after 1 January 1983. The issue at stake in the case was not a claim to benefit under a pension scheme, but the termination of the contract of employment. The judge did not deliver a ruling on the applicability of art. 1637ij of the Civil Code. The employer applied to the judge for the dissolution of the employment relationship on the ground that the relationship would be altered (dissolution on the ground of changes in circumstances).

The *Kantonrechter* ruled that it had to be judged from the working situation whether or not there had been an alteration in the employment relationship.

In this case that had not been established. The fact that the plaintiff opposed the termination of the contract of employment was not a ground for dissolution of the employment relationship. Moreover, the employer's undertaking was a large one. Article 1637ij of the Civil Code was not directly applicable to the procedure for dissolving an employment relationship. Nevertheless, the judge had to take into account the principle of

---

[1]   NJ 1986, 17 and 18.

equal treatment of men and women. The request for dissolution of the employment relationship was refused.

Rechtbank Amsterdam
11 July 1985[1]

PREGNANCY.

The plaintiff had when applying for a job indicated that she was pregnant, but she was nevertheless selected. After she had worked for 10 days she had to report sick because of complications in her pregnancy. The employer terminated the employment relationship on the ground that he had not sufficiently been able to assess the plaintiff during the probationary period.

The Equal Treatment Committee stated that art. 1637ij of the Civil Code could not be circumvented by terminating the employment relationship during the probationary period. However, termination of an employment relationship during the probationary period on the grounds of absence due to complications in the pregnancy was not termination on the grounds of pregnancy and was allowed. In this case there had not been discrimination between men and women.

The plaintiff claimed that the termination of her employment within the probationary period on the grounds of pregnancy was null and void, and claimed payment of wages.

The President of the *Rechtbank* (District Court) held that it was not likely that the plaintiff had been dismissed because of her pregnancy or the complications caused thereby. Within the probationary period the defendant was entitled to terminate the employment at any time. The petition was refused.

Rechtbank Arnhem
30 May 1985[2]
De Haan/Stichting Samenlevingsopbouw

REFUSAL TO ENGAGE BECAUSE OF PREGNANCY.

The plaintiff claimed that she was turned down, when applying for a temporary job (of approximately one year), or dismissed immediately after the contract of employment was concluded. The reason was that she would not be available for work during a period of about three months, due to pregnancy and maternity leave.

---

[1] KG 1985, 232.
[2] Rolno 1984/2151.

The Equal Treatment Committee stated that reference to pregnancy amounted to direct discrimination. Reference to limited availability caused by pregnancy was indirect discrimination. This is justified by the temporary nature and the short term of the employment relationship. There was no breach of art. 1637ij of the Civil Code.

The plaintiff sought the issuing of a written contract of employment and compensation.

The President of the *Rechtbank* (District Court) held that only after the judge had ruled that no contract of employment had been concluded could it be inferred that the defendant had refused to conclude a contract of employment with the plaintiff. Only then could the question arise as to whether the defendant had violated the Equal Treatment Act, and thus had treated the plaintiff unlawfully.

The *Rechtbank* held that it had not been established that the contract of employment was fully concluded. The employer had committed indirect discrimination by referring to family circumstances. Whether there was also direct discrimination could remain undecided. The infringement of art. 1637ij of the Civil Code presented, in principle, an unlawful act. *In casu* this unlawful act was justified by the circumstances: the vacancy had to be filled at short notice; and it was a temporary job for approximately one year. There was no unlawful act. The claim was dismissed.

Ambtenarengerecht Groningen
12 March 1986[1]

DISMISSAL.

A female teaching co-ordinator, working in a prison, informed the management that she had developed a serious attachment to a prisoner. Admittance to the institution was immediately refused. The management was of the opinion that she had concealed a serious relationship for two months. Moreover, she had made her return impossible by informing the staff. The woman was of the opinion that a man, in comparable circumstances, would not have been dismissed, but transferred.

The *Ambtenarengerecht* (Civil Servants' Tribunal) declared the dismissal to be null and void.

The Equal Treatment Committee (civil servants) stated that, according to the Ministry of Justice, in cases like these it had to be considered whether a transfer was sufficient. It was not clear why in this case dismissal would be

---

[1]   GERRITSEN I, p. 99.

necessary. Moreover, the dismissal was null and void according to the *Ambtenarengerecht*. For the Committee it was difficult to avoid the impression that no reasonable solution had been looked for. The fact that the plaintiff was a woman had been a decisive factor. There was direct discrimination.

Kantonrechter Gouda
13 March 1986[1]

JOB NOT SUITABLE FOR A BREADWINNER. REASONS OTHER THAN DISCRIMINATORY ONES DECISIVE IN NOT HIRING.

The plaintiff was turned down for a job in Davos (Switzerland), amongst other reasons because of her family circumstances: her husband would not be able to find a job in Switzerland and there would be no crèche for the child. Furthermore, it would not be easy to live with a family of three on the salary that would be paid for the job which the plaintiff had applied for.

The Equal Treatment Committee held that family circumstances had been a factor in the employer's decision. The Committee, however, could not establish that it had been this factor which accounted for the fact that the plaintiff had not been appointed.

The plaintiff claimed damages under art. 1401 of the Civil Code (unlawful act) and/or conflict with pre-contractual good faith.

The *Kantonrechter* (Cantonal Judge) held that indirect discrimination had resulted from the reference to family circumstances. This was an unlawful act, as a consequence of which the employer was in principle liable for damages. There had been no material damage because there was no causal relationship between the reference to family circumstances and the failure to be selected. The application would equally not have led to the desired appointment if there had been no reference to the plaintiff's family circumstances. Payment of immaterial damages of Hfl 1.00 was ordered.

Kantonrechter 's-Hertogenbosch
27 May 1986[2]

BREADWINNER.

Employees who were considered to be breadwinners received higher pay than other employees. The pay of these other employees could not be raised because the employer was in financial difficulties. The wages were not

---

[1]   *Praktijkgids* 1987, p. 212, No 2667; Rolno 538/85.
[2]   Rolno 2935/85 VT, unreported.

averaged because that would have resulted in the wages of breadwinners being reduced, and this would have been unjust considering their family circumstances.

The Equal Treatment Committee held that the use of the breadwinner concept implied indirect discrimination, because it was, generally speaking, detrimental to women. The consideration that a basic income should be guaranteed to the family was no longer relevant, as a result of a number of measures in the field of secondary incomes. Any reference to the necessity to provide subsistence for children was a reference to family circumstances (and therefore indirect discrimination).

The plaintiff filed a claim for back pay.

The *Kantonrechter* stated that the Equal Pay Act was applicable to claims for wages. The Equal Pay Act was a *lex specialis* with a special judicial process. In this case no Opinion from the Equal Treatment Committee under the Equal Pay Act about the claim for wages had been submitted. The Opinion pursuant to the Equal Treatment Act was older than three months. The claim was dismissed.

President Rechtbank Dordrecht (Summary Proceedings)
11 February 1988[1]
Evers and Evers/van der Giessen-de Noord NV

DISMISSAL.

The defendant had to reduce drastically the size of the workforce. Permission for dismissal had been requested for 52 employees, amongst them eight women. Permits to dismiss were received for 27 employees, five of them women. The other requests were still under consideration.

The plaintiffs complained of discrimination, pursuant to art. 1 of the Equal Treatment Act read together with art. 1637ij of the Civil Code.

They demanded that the defendant be ordered to suspend the requests for permission for dismissal until the Equal Treatment Committee had reached a decision.

The President of the *Rechtbank* (District Court) ruled that the claimants thought that they were unjustly not placed in a group which could possibly be transferred. They failed, however, to meet one of the criteria for transfer (namely, a sick-leave record of not more than 25 per cent and not more often than seven times in the previous year) for placement in that group. If this was true, there was no question of discrimination. Since it was not thought

---

[1]   RvdW/KG 1988, 139.

probable that the Equal Treatment Committee would reach a different view, the director of the GAB (regional labour office, who had to issue the permission for dismissal) was fully qualified to examine the validity of the statements of the parties. The claim was dismissed.

Ambtenarengerecht Amsterdam
30 August 1988[1]

PREFERENTIAL TREATMENT FOR WOMEN.

The Municipality of Amsterdam had a positive action policy.

A woman applied for a job. She was not appointed. The positive action policy was not applied in her case.

The *Ambtenarengerecht* held that neither the woman, nor the man who was eventually appointed, were fully qualified for the job. Therefore they had to be considered as equal applicants. In making the ultimate choice between the candidates, the Municipality had wrongly deviated from its positive action policy, that when there are two equal applicants the female applicant should get preference. The decision under consideration therefore had not been taken after due consideration of the legal requirements.

8.4   DECISIONS ON EQUALITY IN SOCIAL SECURITY[2]

8.4.1   HIGHER COURTS

Centrale Raad van Beroep
1 November 1983[3]

DIRECT DISCRIMINATION.

The WWV (Act on Unemployment Benefits) at the time contained the provision that married women were not entitled to benefits under this Act, unless they were considered to be breadwinners.

The plaintiffs claimed under art. 26 of the International Covenant on Civil and Political Rights and challenged the validity of the provision.

---

1   TAR 1988, 198. See also President of the *Rechtbank* of Amsterdam, 29 November 1988, TAR 1989, 22, *NJCM-Bulletin* 1989, pp 167-180; and President of the *Rechtbank* of Amsterdam, 5 January 1989, TAR 1989, 63.
2   In this part use is made, *inter alia*, of C.M. SJERPS, 'Dames en heren, en dan nu: gelijke behandeling', SMA 1988, p. 306, and of A.W. HERINGA, *NJCM-Bulletin* 1988, p. 98.
3   RSV 1984, 147; *NJCM-Bulletin* 9-1, 1984.

The *Centrale Raad van Beroep* dismissed the claim under art. 26 of the International Covenant because that provision had no direct effect. Social fundamental rights can, generally speaking, only be achieved by degree, by way of legislation and other implementing measures. Distinctive criteria such as those of man/woman and married/single, present in social security rules, which are connected with social structures, could be deemed discriminatory. They could, however, usually only be removed by gradual measures. This, apparently, was also the view of Directive 79/7/EEC of 19 December 1978, which (with a number of exceptions and restrictions) provided that the gradual achievement of the equal treatment principle in the field of social security should take place within six years.

The *Centrale Raad* held that, for the above-mentioned reasons, art. 26 of the International Covenant did not have direct effect in respect of the particular social security issue.

Centrale Raad van Beroep
14 May 1987[1]

DIRECT DISCRIMINATION.

In the *Wet Uitkering Vervolgingsslachtoffers* (Act on Benefits for Victims of Persecution) a direct distinction was made between men and women. The *Centrale Raad* held that this discrimination was in conflict with art. 26 of the International Covenant on Civil and Political Rights. This provision had direct effect from 23 December 1984, when Directive 79/7/EEC came into force.

The plaintiff therefore could only claim benefits as of that date. For the period prior to that date she had no entitlement to benefit. The *Centrale Raad* nevertheless pointed out that 'this does not mean that a revision of the Act should not have an earlier commencing date than' 23 December 1984.

Centrale Raad van Beroep
5 January 1988[2]

The plaintiff's disability benefit based on the AAW (General Disability Act) was stopped from 19 May 1980 because of the fact that she had got married on that date.

The plaintiff argued that the legislation contained a distinction on the ground of sex which was discriminatory and therefore was in conflict with international obligations entered into by the Netherlands.

---

1   RSV 1987, 246; AB 1987, 543.
2   RVS 1988, 104; *NJCM-Bulletin* 1988, p. 98.

The *Raad van Beroep* ruled that art. 26 of the International Covenant on Civil and Political Rights contained independent material law and also was relevant to a social security claim as under discussion. The article might not contain an obligation to give further shape to the acknowledged rights at a national level, but did include the duty, in so far as this (also in the field of social security) has happened, to harmonize the legislation or implementation measures with the article of the Covenant.

No justification based on reasonable and objective grounds which were not related to discrimination based on sex could be found for the fact that the person concerned was disqualified from benefits because she did not meet a requirement which was not imposed on a married man (that is to say the requirement that the disability had set in on or after 1 October 1975), either in the words of the Act – the General Disability Act, as amended by the Act introducing Equal Claims for Benefits *(Wet Invoering Gelijke Uitkeringsrechten voor Mannen en Vrouwen)*[1] – or in the history of the amendment. The disqualification from the disability benefit from the day of the marriage had to be considered direct discrimination on the ground of sex, connected with marital status. This contravened art. 26 of the International Covenant.

There was no reason to deny art. 26 direct effect from the moment the legislature clearly intended to harmonize the disability law with that provision, namely 1 January 1980. Article 26 was sufficiently precise to be relied upon by individuals before national courts in order to prevent the application of any provision contravening that article.

Therefore the provisions of art. IV(3) and art. VI(1) of the Act introducing Equal Claims for Benefits were held to be ineffective as of 19 May 1980.

Centrale Raad van Beroep
7 December 1988[2]

Under the *Algemene Weduwen- en Wezenwet* (AWW: General Act on Benefits for Widows and Orphans) widowers were not entitled to benefits.

A widower nevertheless filed a claim for benefits under the AWW.

The *Centrale Raad* stated that the AWW made an unjustified distinction between men and women.

In the first place, an amendment to the Act by which the unequal treatment of men and women in the AWW was to be removed had been in preparation for some time. Clearly the Government itself thought that there was an unjustified distinction between men and women in the Act.

---

1   Act of 20 December 1979, Stb 1979, 708.
2   RSV 1989, p. 67.

Secondly, there was not always a justification of the unequal treatment in the AWW. In many cases the male partner with children met with as many difficulties as the female partner who became a widow.

Moreover, even if it was assumed that the restriction of claims in the AWW to widows was formerly justifiable, that had not been the case for a considerable time because of changes in the social circumstances.

The *Centrale Raad* stated that when a provision contravened art. 26 of the International Covenant, and when, as was the case here, art. 26 had direct effect, that discrimination had to be removed.

Centrale Raad van Beroep
23 June 1992[1]

The General Disability Act (AAW) contained the provision that, in order to qualify for benefits, a certain income had to have been earned in the year prior to the disability (art. 6, paras (1) and (2)). The *Centrale Raad van Beroep* considered that more women than men would be prejudiced by this rule. In so far as any amount of income had to have been earned, the *Centrale Raad van Beroep* ruled that that requirement was objectively justified, because the Act had as its purpose to insure against loss of income. The level of the income that had to have been earned, however, was unnecessarily high for the achievement of the goal. The provision by which the level of the income is set (art. 6, para. (2)) was therefore indirectly discriminating and in contravention of art. 4 of Directive 79/7/EEC.

8.4.2   COURTS OF APPEAL

Gerechtshof 's-Gravenhage
13 March 1985[2]
The Netherlands/Federatie Nederlandse Vakverenigingen

DIRECT EFFECT OF DIRECTIVE. WHETHER FAILURE TO IMPLEMENT THE DIRECTIVE AN UNLAWFUL ACT.

The President of the *Rechtbank* (District Court) had, in summary proceedings, held that the Netherlands had not fulfilled its duty to repeal laws contrary to the equal treatment principle, *in casu* the WWV (Act on Unemployment Benefits).[3] The WWV denied benefits to married women unless they were considered to be breadwinners. The President stated that this was unlawful. The President ordered the Netherlands to adjust the Act before 1 March 1985.

---

1   *NJCM-Bulletin* 1993, p. 292.
2   NJ 1985, 263.
3   17 January 1985; NJ 1985, 262.

The *Gerechtshof* (Regional Court), on appeal, held that putting national Acts to the test of general principles of law was not permitted by the Netherlands Constitution. Assessing the WWV in accordance with the principle of equal treatment, therefore, was only possible if Directive 79/7/EEC had direct effect. Since it was not clear whether the Directive had direct effect in the period before 24 December 1984, the Court referred to the ECJ for a preliminary ruling.[1]

The *Gerechtshof* also rejected the view that the State had acted unlawfully as against the defendant and especially the female members represented by the defendant by permitting a provision to exist contrary to Directive 79/7/EEC.

8.4.3   LOWER TRIBUNALS

Raad van Beroep Groningen
3 June 1987[2]

This case was about the amending Act[3] which provided for the repeal of art. 13(1)(1) of the WWV (Act on Unemployment Benefits) and enacted a temporary measure. It was argued that the provision whereby the repeal of art. 13(1)(1) was not applicable to an employee who had become unemployed before 23 December 1984, unless he received unemployment benefits under the *Werkloosheidswet* (Unemployment Act) on that date, contravened art. 4 of Directive 79/7/EEC. This was argued to be the case because the provision implied that a woman who was not a breadwinner, but who, if she were a man, would have received WWV benefit on 23 December 1984 which would have continued after 23 December 1984, did not qualify for that benefit after 23 December 1984. The *Raad van Beroep* held this to contravene art. 4 of the Directive. The temporary measure was declared inapplicable. Referring to the judgment of the ECJ of 4 December 1986 the *Raad* arrived at the conclusion that the plaintiff was entitled to benefit (from 23 December 1984) under the same conditions which would apply to a married man in equal circumstances.

Raad van Beroep Amsterdam
29 December 1987[4]
Teuling-Worms/Bedrijfsvereniging voor de chemische industrie

The *Raad van Beroep* held that exceptions to the equal treatment principle should be interpreted in a restrictive manner.

---

1   See *Netherlands* v. *Federatie Nederlandse Vakbeweging*, Case 71/85, [1986] ECR 3855 (ECJ).
2   *NJCM-Bulletin* 12-5 (1987); Prg 1987, p. 37, No 2697.
3   Stb 1985, 230.
4   RSV 1988, 173.

The *Raad* held that justifications for indirect discrimination were such an exception. It should therefore not be readily assumed that there was such a justification. From this point of view the *Raad* considered whether or not the system of increases in benefits for breadwinners in the AAW (General Disability Act) contravened the prohibition of indirect discrimination. It took into account the fact that the AAW contained such exemptions which in the view of the *Raad* were not at all times necessary to guarantee a minimum level of subsistence for beneficiaries with dependants,[1] and, on the other hand, the fact that the system of the AAW was not always appropriate to achieve the objective in question (the guarantee of a minimum benefit). The *Raad* reached the conclusion that the system of increases of benefits for breadwinners in the AAW was indirectly discriminatory against women and as such contravened art. 4 of Directive 79/7/EEC.

Raad van Beroep Haarlem
16 February 1989[2]
Maris/Sociale Verzekeringsbank

The plaintiff had cohabited since 1 October 1984 with a partner. On 4 September 1987 the plaintiff and her partner gave notice of a marriage at the registry office. The marriage was to take place on 1 October.

On 13 September 1987 the plaintiff and her partner had an accident. The plaintiff's partner died on 27 September 1987 as a consequence of the accident.

The plaintiff applied for a widow's pension in connection with the death of the partner. The defendant refused this request on the grounds that the plaintiff was not entitled to benefits under the General Act on Benefits for Widows and Orphans (AWW: *Algemene Weduwen- en Wezenwet*) because she was not married to her partner.

The *Raad van Beroep* stated that the defendant's decision had to be put to the test of art. 26 of the International Covenant on Civil and Political Rights. The *Raad* asked whether the prohibition of discrimination in art. 26 of the International Covenant also concerned discrimination between married and unmarried persons. The *Raad* held that social ideas and developments were such that married couples on the one hand and cohabitants on the other were no longer to be considered unequal cases.

The *Raad* held that the distinction between married and cohabiting couples in art. 8 of the AWW was unequal treatment and as such direct discrimination on the grounds of status as covered by art. 26 of the International Covenant.

---

1 Exempted were, among others, benefits under the WAO (Workers' Disability Act) and supplements to the AAW benefit.
2 No AWW 82/29/Z.

9. DOCUMENTATION

9.1 BIBLIOGRAPHY

9.1.1 BOOKS AND REPORTS

ASSCHER-VONK, I.P.,
— *Ondernemingsraad en gelijke behandeling*, Samsom uitgeverij, Alphen aan den Rijn, 1986.
— *Toegang tot de Dienstbetrekking*, Alphen aan den Rijn, 1989.

ASSCHER-VONK, I.P., and WENTHOLT, K., *Wet gelijke behandeling van mannen en vrouwen*, Deventer, 1994.

BOELENS, L., and VELDMAN, A., *Gelijkwaardige arbeid, gelijk gewaardeerd*, Utrecht, 1993.

EVENHUIS, C.H.S., *De Zykant van het gelijk*, Zwolle, 1991.

FASE, W. (editor), *Gelijke behandeling van vrouw en man in de sociale zekerheid*, Kluwer, Deventer, 1986.

GERRITSEN, A.M., 'Rechtspraak gelijke behandeling m/v 1975-1986', *NJCM-boekerij*, 1987.

GOLDSCHMIDT, J.E., *et al.*, 'Vrouw en recht', Stichting *NJCM-boekerij*, Leiden, 1984.

GOVERS, A.W., and BOSSCHER, A.E., *Gelijkheid van vrouw en man in het Europees sociaal recht, Geschriften van de Vereniging voor arbeidsrecht*, No 6, Samsom uitgeverij, Alphen aan den Rijn, 1981.

VAN DER GRINTEN, W.C., *Discriminatie en burgerlijk recht*, afscheidscollege Nijmegen, 1984.

GROENENDIJK, C.A., *Heeft wetgeving tegen discriminatie effect?*, Zwolle, 1986.

JASPERS, A.PH., and VAN KLEINWEE, M.T.C., *Gelijke behandeling, je goed recht? Een onderzoek naar het funktioneren van de Commissie gelijke behandeling van mannen en vrouwen bij de arbeid*, Ministerie van Sociale Zaken en Werkgelegenheid, 's-Gravenhage, 1985.

NOORDAM, F.M., *Inleiding Sociale-Zekerheidsrecht*, Deventer, 1994.

SLOOT, B., *Positieve discriminatie*, Zwolle, 1986.

VIERDAG, E.W., *The concept of discrimination in international law*, Den Haag, 1973.

VAN DER WEELE, J.J., *Wet Gelijke Behandeling van Mannen en Vrouwen*, Sociaal- en arbeidsrechtelijke reeks No 13, Kluwer, Deventer, 1983.

9.1.2 ARTICLES AND NOTES

Anonymous: 'Nieuwe wetgeving', Nemesis 1987, p. 229.

ASSCHER-VONK, I.P.,
— 'Gelijke rechtspositie voor man en vrouw in het arbeidsrecht', SMA 1977, p. 387.
— 'Vorderingen tot naleving van de Wet Gelijke Behandeling van Mannen en Vrouwen', SMA 1980, p. 503.
— 'Het voorontwerp van een wet gelijke behandeling: de sanctionering', NJB 1982, p. 385.
— 'Discriminatie en burgerlijk recht', NJB 1984, p. 908.
— 'Positieve Actieplannen', SMA 1985, p. 823.

—   'Gelijke behandeling in de sociale zekerheid', *NJCM-Bulletin* 1985, p. 275.
—   'Toegang tot de dienstbetrekking via gelijke behandeling', in *Schetsen voor Bakels*, Deventer, 1987.
—   'Wijziging van het BBA', NJB 1987, p. 235.
—   'Gevolgen van het Dekker-arrest voor de sanctionering van gelijke behandelingsregels', SMA 1993, p. 186.
—   'Transformation of Civil Law Sanctions', in M. VERWILGHEN (Ed.), *Access to Equality between Men and Women*, Louvain-la-Neuve, 1993.

VAN BOKHOVEN, S., 'De Zaak van Dam: een discriminatoir ontslag', Nemesis 1985, pp 112-120.

BOSKAMP, V., 'Voorkeurs behandeling: heldhaftig, vastberaden en barmhartig?', SMA 1989, p. 416.

GOVERS, A.W., 'Gelijke behandeling in de sociale zekerheid, wat doet de rechter?', *NJCM-Bulletin* 1985, p. 365.

HEERMA VAN VOSS, G., 'Discriminatie en ontslag van buitenlandse zeelieden: de zaak Nedlloyd', *NJCM-Bulletin* 1985, p. 187.

HERINGA, A.W., and DE ZWART, T., 'Noot bij CRvB 1-11-1983', *NJCM-Bulletin* 1984, p. 23.

HERINGA, A.W.,
—   'Noot bij Raad van beroep Groningen 2-5-1985', *NJCM-Bulletin* 1985, p. 546.
—   'Noot bij RvB Groningen 3-6-1987', *NJCM-Bulletin* 1987, p. 399.
—   'Noot bij Centrale Raad van Beroep 14-5-1987', *NJCM-Bulletin* 1987, pp 465 and 480.
—   'Noot bij CRvB 5 januari 1988 en RvB Amsterdam 29 december 1987', *NJCM-Bulletin* 1988, p. 98.

DE KOK, F.J.C.M., 'Sexe-discriminatie en bewijslast', *NJCM-Bulletin* 1984, p. 381.

JASPERS, T., and WIELE, J., 'Rechters of Commissie?', Nemesis 1987, p. 255.

JASPERS, A.PH.C.M., 'Selectief werkgelegenheidsbeleid: geoorloofde bescherming of discriminatie', in *Schetsen voor Bakels*, Deventer, 1987, p. 105.

JASPERS, SCHIPPERS and SIEGERS, 'Klagen bij de Commissie gelijke behandeling', SMA 1987, p. 75.

JESSURUN D'OLIVEIRA, H.U., 'Onderscheid naar nationaliteit: Discriminatie?', *NJCM-Bulletin* 1984, p. 327.

LOENEN, T., 'Gelijke behandeling van mannen en vrouwen 0- voorwaarden voor ontslag', *NJCM-Bulletin* 1986, p. 324.

PRECHAL, S., 'Over vrouwen die na hun zestigste niet meer mochten werken', Nemesis 1986, p. 127.

SJERPS, C.M.,
—   'Voldoet de adviesaanvrage stelselherziening aan de derde EG-Richtlijn inzake gelijke behandeling in de sociale zekerheid?', SMA 1984, p. 81.
—   'Tellen en tellen is twee. Enkele opmerkingen over het gebruik van statistische gegevens bij het aantonen van indirecte sexe-discriminatie', SMA 1985, p. 362.
—   'Dames en heren, en dan nu: gelijke behandeling! Of: hoe verder na de recente uitspraken van Raden en Centrale Raad van Beroep', SMA 1988, p. 306.

VERMEULEN, B.P., *Praktijkgids*, 1988, No 2886.

9.2   INFORMATION

9.2.1   USEFUL ADDRESSES

Commissie Gelijke Behandeling
Postbus 16001
3500 DA Utrecht

INDEX